THE ST. CLARE PRAYER BOOK

THE *St. Clare* PRAYER BOOK

Listening for God's Leading

BY
JON M. SWEENEY

PARACLETE PRESS
BREWSTER, MASSACHUSETTS

The St. Clare Prayer Book: Listening for God's Leading

2007 First Printing

Copyright © 2007 by Jon M. Sweeney

ISBN 13: 978-1-55725-504-4

Scripture quotations designated NJB are taken from the New Jerusalem Bible, published and copyright © 1985 by Darton, Longman & Todd Ltd. and Doubleday, a division of Random House Inc., and used by permission of the publishers.

Scripture quotations designated NRSV are taken from the New Revised Standard Version Bible, copyright © 1989 by the Division of Christian Education of the National Council of the Churches of Christ in the United States of America, and are used by permission. All rights reserved.

Scripture quotations designated REB are taken from the Revised English Bible, copyright © Oxford University Press and Cambridge University Press 1989, and are used by permission.

Scripture translations used are as follows unless noted in the Scripture reference: Gospels—NJB; Psalms—The Book of Common Prayer (1979); Songs, Canticles, and Epistles from the Old and New Testaments—NRSV and REB.

Library of Congress Cataloging–in–Publication Data

Sweeney, Jon M., 1967-
  The St. Clare prayer book : listening for God's leading / by Jon M. Sweeney.
      p. cm.
  Includes bibliographical references and index.
  ISBN-13: 978-1-55725-513-6
  1. Clare, of Assisi, Saint, 1194-1253. 2. Meditations.
  3. Prayers. I. Title.
BX4700.C6S94 2007
242'.802--dc22   2006031318

10 9 8 7 6 5 4 3 2 1

Published by Paraclete Press
Brewster, Massachusetts
www.paracletepress.com
Printed in the United States of America

CONTENTS

V
APPENDICES

I

THE PRAYER LIFE
of St. Clare of Assisi

*B*Y ALL ACCOUNTS, she was an attractive and lively girl, smart and strong-willed. Her conversion to religious life culminated one night as she snuck away from her parents' home on the eastern edge of Assisi and joined St. Francis and the friars at Portiuncula, a tiny chapel, down in the valley below town. She was eighteen years old and had spent several years questioning her family's ideas of who she should marry and who she would become. She chose to run away—and run toward—the enigmatic Francis, who had upset the town several years before with his similar conversion.

But just as St. Clare began her religious life dramatically, the next four plus decades saw her spend most of her time in prayer. She was like a mother to her sisters, counseling them on why and how to pray, and helping them with their questions about the spiritual life. She possessed a quiet power that was respected by all who came to know her. She communicated often with popes, cardinals, and women and men around Europe about what it means to be Christian. Clare of Assisi was the most important woman of her day, even though she spent most of her life behind bars.

The bars were known as a grille, which separated St. Clare and her sisters both symbolically and physically from all visitors who would come to their little convent just outside Assisi. Even the priest who would hear their confessions and administer the sacraments was separated by the grille from the Poor Clares.

It is behind that grille that St. Clare found her true freedom in Christ—a freedom to explore a relationship with God that was unencumbered by societal expectations. She used prayer books, and she memorized many of her prayers. The little book you hold in your hands would probably embarrass her, but she would also understand exactly how to use it.

We pick up prayer books when we realize that we need something to stimulate our devotion to God. For many of us, prayer is our lifeboat, but we still find ourselves treading water from time to time. The unique vision and spiritual depth of St. Clare's prayers and prayer life will open for you new opportunities and paths for knowing God.

ᔕᓚ

St. Clare's prayers are very rarely collected in books. She is often overshadowed by her more famous friend and mentor, St. Francis. Evelyn Underhill once referred to Clare as "the hidden spring" of Franciscan spirituality, an apt description because Clare's wisdom was a spring for Francis and the first generation of Franciscans. It is only in recent years that we have come to discover it.

St. Clare is a different sort of saint from the ones we may be accustomed to spending time with. Her life and spirituality bring to a life of faith something different that is both relevant today and unique among her more famous contemporaries.

By outward appearances, her life was drab compared to the colorful lives of such women as Catherine of Siena and Hildegard of Bingen. Catherine scolded popes and emperors, and Hildegard composed mystical music and theological texts. Both women had a wide range of interests and influence in the world of politics and power, in contrast to Clare, whose life was mostly hidden except to her spiritual brothers and sisters.

St. Clare's stature has also been hampered by the pious descriptions that grew up around her legends. This began with the biography that Thomas of Celano wrote just after her death as part of the process of canonizing her. Every writer since the 1250s has had to make decisions about what is history in Thomas's accounts and what is simply good storytelling in the life of a saint. Many misinterpretations have persisted through the centuries, and sometimes writers have made her sound so pure as to become more angelic than human.

For example, in the early twentieth century, Father Cuthbert wrote these saccharine sentences in his study of St. Clare: "One must be grossly lacking in spiritual perception not to recognize in the story of her life . . . the pure spirituality which was the atmosphere in which her mind and heart had their being. In her it is evident no ordinary earthliness found place, but all was consecrated by a purity staid with the constant vision and love of the heavenly life." He would like us to believe that Clare never faced temptation, never doubted her vocation, and that human emotions such as anger, frustration, boredom, and sadness failed to affect her prayer life. The opposite was true, and that is why Clare speaks so profoundly to us today.

Twenty-seven years separated St. Francis's and St. Clare's deaths. In other words, she had better than a quarter century to live out the ideals of Francis in her own ways. The two great saints of Assisi shared much in common: They each began their religious lives with dramatic gestures of separation from worldly values and self-conscious identification with the person of Christ—but Clare's subsequent spirituality became strong, wise, and quiet in ways that differentiate her from her mentor. Where Francis usually sought to jolt people into understanding truth directly and experientially, Clare grew slowly and deeply into wisdom. As a result, it takes more time and patience to learn from Clare than it does from Francis.

St. Clare and her first sisters in religious life were bound by the traditional vow of stability, and in contrast to Francis and the first friars, stability meant a cloistered life. The life of Clare was completely centered in a small community of women in the former Assisan church of San Damiano. For forty-one years, Clare lived almost every moment of life within the walls of that church-turned-leper hospital-turned-monastery. The prospect of such a circumspect existence has caused one writer to recently refer to San Damiano as "Clare's *Prison*." But it wasn't so.

Despite society's ideas about the roles of women, who were seen as the "second sex," inferior to men, St. Clare formed a way of Christian living that was deepened through separation from men and from most of society around her. Spiritual formation went on behind that grille, and it was women transformed who then went out into the world to help the sick, give to the poor, pray for the needs of others, and found new houses for more women to do the same.

St. Francis himself desired that St. Clare spend most of her days within the monastery; he believed that her calling was different from his own. In that era, men and women outside of religious orders did not mingle unless they were married or were blood relatives. Men did not visit with women unless a chaperone was present; men did not even look upon women unless their intentions were clearly stated; and the men and women of the Franciscan movement could not work side by side.

However, in that era when women outside marriage and cloister were usually regarded merely as temptations to men, St. Clare became a not-so-hidden spring to the men around her: St. Francis and the other friars who came to rely on her after Francis's death, as well as cardinals and even popes. As one contemporary Poor Clare sister has described it, "[Clare's] conscience was formed by a theology which viewed women as embodiments of evil inclined to lust and sensuality." She overcame society's expectations for her and became one of the most important religious leaders of her day.

ST. CLARE AND ST. FRANCIS SIDE BY SIDE

St. Francis of Assisi was peripatetic in his spirituality and in his prayer life. Francis was God's juggler, an innovator, a passionate, creative personality, and these qualities come through in the few descriptions and depictions left to us. He was small, strong, and always on the move. G. K. Chesterton explains:

> All his life was a series of plunges and scampers; darting after the beggar, dashing naked into the woods, tossing himself into the strange ship, hurling himself into the Sultan's tent and offering to hurl himself into the fire. In appearance he must have been like a thin brown skeleton autumn leaf dancing eternally before the wind; but in truth it was he that was the wind.

These qualities carried over into St. Francis's life of prayer. In many respects, Francis "made it up as he went along," as one might say today—which is what made the early years of his movement creative and energizing for thousands of converts. We know from that collection of tales, *The Little Flowers*, that in the early days Francis would sometimes gather his followers together and ask them with fervor to open their mouths as the Spirit of God so moved them. Thus was their simple prayer session, composed of the movings of the Spirit as a Quaker meeting might be today. After each had spoken as the Spirit had prompted him, Francis once summarized: "Dear brothers, give thanks to God, who has willed that by the mouths of babes should be revealed the treasures of heavenly wisdom."

In St. Clare's heart were the ideals that made St. Francis's bold actions in the world make sense. As Francis and the friars were walking all over Italy and Europe, Clare and the sisters were deepening the same sense of excitement and enthusiasm, primarily among and within themselves, as well as in their local settings. Many communities of Poor Clares were formed beyond Assisi, including one in Florence headed by Clare's sister Agnes, but Clare always remained put. Clare's depth and constancy of prayer gave rise to an interior life that was different from Francis's and that expresses itself in Clare's prayers. She became known throughout

Italy as a woman of profound wisdom. As the cleric who wrote the papal bull for Clare's canonization explained it, "Clare was concealed, yet her life was revealed; Clare kept silence, yet her reputation cried aloud; she was hidden in a cell, but known throughout the towns."

The spirit of St. Clare's written prayers is as full of joy and charity as St. Francis's, but Clare's prayer life was also more rooted in community and all of its challenges. One imagines that Francis would have been a difficult companion: coming and going at all hours, changing direction and priorities often and at an instant, never thinking about the future. Indeed, he would have made a lousy husband except to Lady Poverty! But Clare was different. She was a deep, ready source of wisdom—a well to Francis's river. Clare developed a form of Franciscan spirituality that was true to the spirit of Francis, while deepening it in various, new directions.

Even the daily work of her hands showed St. Clare as one who brought spiritual strength to others who were more visible. From the first days, every Franciscan was to have manual work of some kind, in addition to prayer and other activities. Behind the walls of San Damiano, Clare's work was embroidery. She embroidered fine altar cloths—the kind that are used during the Mass on the high altar and on which the host is set. This is the sort of work that St. Francis would have never done himself, but upon which he surely relied. Tradition also has it that Clare created the cloth-shoes for Francis's tender feet after he was blessed with the stigmata.

It was during these extended periods of silence, manual work, and care for the needs of others that St. Clare became famous for intercessory prayer. Her intercessions were highly valued by popes, cardinals, the friars, and St. Francis himself. All of these men would send word to Clare, asking for her intercession and, often, for her received wisdom. She also had a unique ability to bring joy to others. Clare served Francis in this way when he rediscovered the gift of song in her garden at San Damiano. It was the last time that they were together, as Francis stopped for a time at San Damiano on his way to Rieti to see a physician. Clare made a special place for him in her garden, and it was in that place and spirit that Francis broke out of a depression that was ailing him and wrote his famous vernacular song, *Canticle of the Creatures.*

St. Clare was also the first woman to write her own Rule for religious life. Before her—and even for much of her own religious life—men wrote the Rules for women. The Dominican sisters, who were closest to the Poor Clares both geographically and chronologically, had rules against laughing in choir, or making someone else laugh; eating without permission of the abbess; any subtle rebellion in word or deed; and much more.

Penalties for breaking these rules were spelled out in detail. Flogging was common, as was being required to humiliate oneself by eating bread and water while kneeling before the rest of the community. In contrast, Clare's Rule was a disappointment to the disciplinarians. She sent the message to her sisters and to the Church authorities who approve monastic Rules—not that Franciscans were not serious or strict (because Francis and Clare could be both)—but that to be a Franciscan was a decision made each day, voluntarily for Christ. The spiritual life is not a path of renunciations.

St. Clare's life of prayer is perhaps best illumined by a metaphor of yeast and bread first suggested by Christ in the Gospel of Matthew, and then repeated by Evelyn Underhill a century ago. In *The School of Charity*, Underhill explains:

> The leavening of meal must have seemed to ancient men a profound mystery, and yet something on which they could always depend. Just so does the supernatural enter our natural life, working in the hiddenness, forcing the new life into every corner and making the dough expand. If the dough were endowed with consciousness, it would not feel very comfortable while the yeast was working. Nor, as a rule, does our human nature feel very comfortable under the transforming action of God.

Sometimes we don't stand still long enough to know the creative action of God working in us through prayer as yeast works in dough. Clare did.

The "hiddenness" of St. Clare was the very source of her wisdom and strength. Her spirituality is full of subtlety and an understanding of the difficulties of being Christian, but she paves the way for us through the habits of a deliberate life of prayer—one where we don't do all of the work ourselves. It is as if the human body remains the same size just as Christ begins to leaven and take fuller shape within it.

ST. CLARE'S LIFE OF PRAYER

In the legends passed down to us about St. Clare, there are many stories of her prayer life as a child. As with all hagiographical texts, we should take these stories with a slight grain of salt, but nevertheless, they can at least point us in the right direction of understanding how and why and where she prayed.

Modeling St. Clare's *Life* after those of other great saints, Thomas of Celano portrays her childhood as devout, sober, and full of distinction from those around her. We have no stories of Clare that depict her childhood as anything approaching typical; she appears to have been one of those children that is serious from the start. Thomas writes that "she delighted in attending holy prayer regularly" and "little by little attained a heavenly life." He compares her to the Desert Fathers and Mothers of ancient Christian tradition when he writes that Clare did not have access to rosary beads as a girl, and so she counted her Our Fathers by casting pebbles aside one by one. She "attached little value to worldly objects," Thomas explains, and "wore a hair shirt underneath her small, precious clothes." All of these references are ways that medieval writers would tell the story of one of their contemporaries in the terms of, and with allusions to, the lives of previous saints. In fact, when Thomas writes about Clare on her deathbed, he compares her to the Virgin Mary. He says that the suffering of Clare's last days was like what Simeon had prophesied to Mary about the Christ Child: "Look, he is destined for the fall and for the rise of many in Israel, destined to be a sign that is opposed—and a sword will pierce your soul too."

It is in St. Clare's adolescence that we first come to see who she would become as a woman of God. Unlike the unquestioning child of Thomas of Celano's early storytelling, Clare shows signs of being a contrarian teenager, full of doubts and questions. There were times when she disobeyed her parents as well as her priest and bishop. Her conversion, in fact, relies on this sort of willful disobedience.

St. Clare did not want to follow the traditional course of a girl from a good family: marriage and children. She observed the conversion of St. Francis and began listening to the Holy Spirit, who had other plans for her life. How it must have surprised and possibly disappointed her parents when she turned away from what they had planned for her! Clare's conversion—on that first night flight to Portiuncula—actually began the morning beforehand, on Palm Sunday, 1212. That morning, during an elaborate and traditional service with all of Assisi in attendance, Clare distinguished herself from all of the other girls in town by refusing to show herself as an eligible woman waiting for the proper marriage match and blessing. She refused to stand to present herself to the bishop for his blessing, as was the fashion of all unmarried girls in town on that special day. This rebuff would have been felt by her parents, as well, who were probably embarrassed by it. At that point, Clare's tender jaw was surely and firmly set, matching a mind and heart already looking in another direction.

Thus began the religious life of St. Clare. It was the stuff of great films. But then what followed were four, quiet decades of deepening experience in prayer. For Clare, it was necessary to leave the secular world in order truly to live in the spiritual world. The same is not true for all of us, today. For many of us, these spiritual riches are ready and waiting, regardless of where we find ourselves and where we live.

There are other, little details about St. Clare's manners and methods of praying that are helpful to understand at the outset of our own praying with her. For instance, Thomas of Celano tells us that Clare often sought the solitude of praying alone late into the night, after the last evening office of Compline. She cried often while praying, an experience that was not unusual for medieval mystics.

Thomas also explains that St. Clare was like a mother to her spiritual sisters. She would sometimes wake up early and would quietly, through the lighting of the lamps and other more subtle means, arouse the younger sisters to pray with her. On other occasions, Clare would intentionally wake up first and rouse the house by ringing a bell for all of the sisters to come to the first office of prayer. Thomas adds this commentary: "There was no place for timidity, no place for idleness, where a quick reproof prodded lazy souls to prayer and service of the Lord." She acted unreservedly as her sisters' spiritual mother when it came to teaching them about prayer. Similarly, when one of her sisters needed healing, she would lay herself at the sister's feet and attempt to caress away the pain as a good mother might do.

St. Clare also practiced visual meditation, a common practice during the late Middle Ages. We have accounts of her doing this in various ways. At times, she would imagine as she lay prostrate facedown on the floor that she was kissing Jesus' feet. Later, Thomas says that she meditated on the Cross to such a degree that she felt the devil strike her on the jaw. At another time, she spent twenty-four hours in a meditative state, feeling as if she were nailed to the cross with Christ; she finally had to be roused by one of her sisters at San Damiano, who used Francis's injunction that Clare may not go a day without food of some kind, in order to bring her back to her senses.

In her meditative practices, St. Clare also prayed at times a series of short prayers taught to her by St. Francis called "The Office of the Five Wounds of Christ" (see p. 141). It is easy to imagine Clare visualizing herself with Jesus in the Garden of Gethsemane, determined to stay awake and pray with him, but also crying beside him. She easily would have understood the poignant African-American spiritual "Were You There When They Crucified My Lord?"

THE FOUNDATION FOR
ST. CLARE'S PRAYERS

St. Clare's life of prayer was built upon a varied foundation. Saints are always constructing on the spiritual work of those saints who have gone before them. For Clare, the building blocks were the teachings of St. Francis, the Old and New Testaments, and the Office of the Feast of St. Agnes of Rome (a fourth-century martyr), whose life and example were meaningful to Clare's understanding of women's spirituality in an age when men so clearly dominated most aspects of everyday life. It was in the spirit of St. Agnes that Clare was fond of quoting from Matthew 13: "The kingdom of Heaven is like treasure hidden in a field which someone has found; he hides it again, goes off in his joy, sells everything he owns and buys the field. Again, the kingdom of Heaven is like a merchant looking for fine pearls; when he finds one of great value he goes and sells everything he owns and buys it."

The primary sources for understanding the spirituality and prayer life of St. Clare are relatively few. Most important, we have Clare's writings: four letters written to Agnes of Prague (the king of Bohemia's daughter who refused arranged marriages to both Emperor Frederick II and King Henry III of England in order to become a Poor Clare in Prague), and one other letter to a woman of influence who chose the religious life (Ermentrude of Bruges); Clare's Rule and Testament; and her final blessing, as recorded by Thomas of Celano in the already-mentioned text, *The Legend of St. Clare*. In total, Clare's writings amount to twenty-two pages in the most recent, authoritative edition.

Another essential component to St. Clare's prayer life was the repetition of praying the Divine Office each day. This form of prayer was inherited from ancient Judaism by the first Christians. The Hebrew psalmists were fond of praying what are sometimes called "the hours" at fixed times throughout the day; as Psalm 119 says, "Seven times a day do I praise you." Clare and her sisters were faithful keepers of these *hours*.

St. Clare prayed the Divine Office more regularly than did St. Francis. Francis was committed to praying the hours, in the manner of monks, but his spirituality was also one of continual pilgrimage following Christ, and as such, he sometimes found it difficult to keep to the regularity of the practice. Clare would not have had that problem.

St. Clare was also probably better educated than Francis. We know that her mother was deeply religious herself, sometimes traveling on pilgrimages to major sites in Europe, and we know that Clare's family was wealthy, offering more educational opportunities and more encouragement at home than Francis would have enjoyed. Her writings show great subtlety as well as a thorough knowledge of Latin. She—and many of her spiritual sisters—would have prayed the Psalter in Latin, its ancient phrases forming the backbone of a religious life. Certain key verses were known by all baptized Christians, even the uneducated, in the same way that nursery rhymes were once known by our parents. Just as a child of the last century might have gone to bed with "I see the moon, and the moon sees me; God bless the moon, and God bless me"—so, too, in Clare's day, many children would associate phrases from the Psalms with the end of the day: "I will bless the LORD who gives me counsel; my heart teaches me, night after night" (16:7). Similarly, as children a generation ago may have woken up to "Donkey, donkey, old and gray, open your mouth and gently bray. Lift your ears and blow your horn to wake the world this sleepy morn"— children in Clare's family home would have known "Be joyful in the LORD, all you lands; serve the LORD with gladness and come before his presence with a song" (100:1) as a way to rise in the morning.

Late medieval religious life was rich with the rhythms and phrasings of psalms, and so were St. Clare's prayers. Psalm 51, for example, was used most every day as a prayer of confession (as it is in the weekly liturgy that follows), and Psalm 8 each Christmas. The Scriptures were read and prayed in Latin, a language much better known to the spiritually minded at that time than the vernacular. St. Francis actually created some of the first vernacular songs and prayers to God, and he is credited by scholars as the very first Italian poet for his famous *Canticle of the Creatures*.

Like St. Francis, St. Clare knew the importance of spiritual reading, and many of her prayers resemble those of great saints who came before her. What confused Francis and Clare was how to use reading for spiritual guidance and edification without becoming too dependent on prayer books. Both Francis and Clare must have known St. Jerome's early medieval instruction against idleness in the religious life: "Be sure to always have holy reading at hand. Look at it when sleep steals upon you and let the sacred page hold up your drooping head." But, both Francis and Clare were hesitant to own prayer books; they both believed that books could too often become crutches to real spiritual learning and engagement in daily life. There are many stories of Francis urging his brother friars not to own their own books, and Clare seems to have carried on this tradition after his death. "*I* am a breviary! *I* am a breviary!" Francis once urged a young novice, in a fruitless attempt to convince him that books are not so much for owning as they are for changing one's life.

While in medieval culture prayer books often became merely decorative or were used superstitiously or perfunctorily, the purer purpose toward which St. Francis and St. Clare called people was the prayer of the heart. The words of books—more than the object of the book itself—are what matter to this sort of prayer in the heart. In England during Clare's era, it was common for a woman to own a copy of the *Life of St. Margaret* simply because expectant women were instructed to clutch the book to their breast during childbirth for protection from harm. It was also common for upper class women to be read to, rather than to read on their own. Chaucer's character Criseyde, for instance, listens with other ladies to tales of Thebes in *Troilus and Criseyde*. Similarly, elaborate Books of Hours would sit on the tables of ladies' dressing rooms, where the ladies would hear edifying words read aloud to them while they were dressing. A woman of Clare's standing in the community most likely said her prayers aloud far more often than she read them. So-called aural reading was once considered a refined substitution for visual reading. But also, both women and men of the Middle Ages believed that to say prayers out loud was one further step toward speaking with, and praying to, the heart. Clare was always praying aloud with her sisters, reminding herself all the while of the truth of prayer words.

ABOVE ALL, JESUS

One of the most important features of St. Clare's prayer life was her absorption in the person of Jesus. Clare's life with Christ was a love story of the highest order. She never fell in love with St. Francis—as novels and Hollywood have supposed—but she did fall in love with Jesus. As many other medieval women mystics would later do, Clare spoke often of Jesus in language that might today be reserved only for words used between physical lovers; it is language that reminds us of the Song of Solomon from the Hebrew Scriptures and of the ways in which love between lovers can be metaphors for the relationship with Christ. Francis had earlier taken Lady Poverty as his "spouse," and so Clare's marriage to Christ made perfect sense within her own religious context.

However, as St. Clare speaks of loving Jesus, she also speaks of loving God the Father, and of the Holy Spirit's love within her. Her expressions of love for and marriage with Christ differ from those of later mystics in this regard. Clare's prayer, inasmuch as it was mystical, was always Trinitarian, focused on the full Christian understanding of God in three persons. This is important to note simply because other medieval mystics were sometimes excessive in one or another direction.

St. Clare always speaks of God as Trinity and views her relationship to God in Christ through the love felt within by the Holy Spirit. St. Francis was actually the one who initially set Clare on this course. In his guidelines for Clare and her sisters—published for posterity by Clare herself in chapter 6 of her Rule—Francis explains that the relationship of Clare to Christ should be as "daughter and servant," and it is the Holy Spirit who is actually likened to her spouse. Francis emphasizes that love for the poor Christ of the cross is deepened in us by the coming of the Holy Spirit as the unifying force of God the Father's love and the Church.

St. Clare echoed these words of St. Francis again and again, in varying metaphor, as she instructed St. Agnes of Prague. With glorious language, Clare uses the following allusions to the Trinity at the beginning of the fourth letter to Agnes:

> To her who is . . . bride of the Lamb . . . servant of Christ . . . handmaid of His handmaids . . . may you sing a new song . . . before the throne of God the Father and follow the Lamb wherever He goes. . . . I delight with you in the joy of the Holy Spirit.

Blessed Angela of Foligno, a prominent Third Order Franciscan, echoed the Franciscan idea of understanding that marriage to Christ is through the Holy Spirit. She recorded having heard these words from God once while on the road between Spello and Assisi: "I am the Holy Spirit, who has come to you to bring you consolation as you have never before tasted. I will be within you and very few of those who are with you will be able to perceive it. I will keep you company and will speak with you at all times. . . . Bride and daughter, you are sweet to Me."

The mystic is as uncommon in Christianity today as it was in Clare's day. But the goals of the mystic are the goals of faith, even when they are expressed in language that is more vivid and pictorial than we might normally be accustomed to. In the last century, Teilhard de Chardin once prayed, "When you stretched out nets to imprison me . . . thrilled with greater joy than when you offered me wings . . . the only element I hanker after in your gifts is the fragrance of your power over me, and the touch of your hand upon me. . . . What exhilarates us human creatures more than freedom . . . is the joy of finding and surrendering . . . the rapture of being possessed." Such is the mystical goal of any Christian, and it fairly represents how Clare felt about Jesus.

THE WISDOM OF MEDITATION

We know that St. Clare spent hours most days in prayer, as did St. Francis. Much of this prayer was contemplative, not vocal. Clare spent little time asking God for things or favors in her prayers. Instead, she spent time *with* Christ, in a quiet, listening relationship that is in itself, without words, prayer. Most of what Clare would have called prayer we today would simply call meditation, or contemplative prayer, or Centering Prayer.

Contemplative life was an important part of St. Clare's dedication to poverty. Both she and St. Francis sought to be voluntarily poor in terms of money and other resources, and they also worked to be poor in spirit, as Jesus described this way of poverty in the Sermon on the Mount. This sort of poverty involved meeting Christ in the simplest, most bare and direct of ways.

There was plenty of spiritual teaching about meditation at this time in Assisi and elsewhere. In fact, several years after the death of St. Clare, the then minister-general of the Franciscans, Bonaventure, wrote to the Poor Clares with advice in these subtle matters. He urged them to "descend" into prayer through stillness and meditation in ways that Clare had already understood:

Return to yourself; enter into your heart;
ponder what you were, are, should have been,
called to be; . . . meditate in your heart; let
your spirit brood. Plow this field, work on
yourself; strive for freedom within, the freedom that leads to relationship with God,
realizing that God will never force us to love
him; . . . if you are not able to understand
(and accept) your own self, you will not be
able to understand (or accept) what is
beyond you.

It is clear that St. Clare spent a great deal of
time in contemplation with God because she
frequently spoke of these sorts of techniques in
her writings. In the third letter to Agnes of
Prague, for instance, Clare urged her to

Place your mind before the mirror of eternity.
Place your soul in the brilliance of heaven.
Place your heart in the figure of the divine
substance.
Transform your entire self into the image of
the Godhead so that you too may feel and
taste the hidden sweetness that God has
reserved for his lovers.

Clare adds a certain poetry to the theological
teachings that would come later from
Bonaventure. These are the specific instructions

from one experienced meditator to another, offering paths of contemplative reflection, each of which one might spend days on end (or longer!) pursuing.

St. Clare was a down-to-earth mystic. Her power of concentration was intense, but hers was a mysticism that had feet and intelligence, in addition to heart. Clare's always practical mystic voice often stands in contrast to those of other medieval mystics.

THE POWER OF INTERCESSION

St. Clare's prayer life was often focused on intercession for the needs of others. These were times when she would appeal to God for the physical, spiritual, and emotional needs of those around her. Naturally, these occasions are not well-chronicled, but we know that Clare's prayers resulted in many answers to prayer. We know that St. Francis often asked Clare's advice in serious matters and for her prayers on his behalf. One story from *The Little Flowers* explains how Francis was doubting his vocation. He was drawn to a life of contemplation and wondering whether or not he was supposed to live more like a hermit. Francis counseled with Clare and with Father Sylvester, the first priest to join the Order and also a renowned contemplative, asking them to pray to God on his behalf, asking God for guidance in the matter of Francis's vocation. Both Sylvester and Clare returned the verdict that Francis was doing as God wanted of him— just as Christ had wanted of the first disciples— to practice his vocation in and among the people of his town and beyond.

Pope Gregory IX, too, was said to rely on St. Clare implicitly, regarding her intercession on his behalf as a chief source of God's wisdom for his life. Some early texts say that Pope Gregory would often write a letter to Clare, explaining his trial or need, and that he would later tangibly experience her spiritual help.

Most important, St. Clare helped her sisters and was the mother of prayer at San Damiano. They turned to her daily for spiritual nourishment in the same way that women in various parts of the world still visit a well each day for water. For them, Clare was a well of wisdom. Her wisdom was hard-won over many trials, decisions, and hours spent forming the habit of words and patterns of communicating with God. She was a deep well, a reservoir of faith and sustenance for other people. We often turn to the saints as intercessors for us to God, and Clare is indeed the saint to whom many turn frequently. Her spirituality matches the metaphor of a well just as an ever-moving river may best capture St. Francis. In her meditation and her prayer, Clare went down deep and often, listening for God's leading.

N.ERICHSEN.

II
PRAYING ALONGSIDE
St. Clare

*S*T. CLARE wrote at the end of her first letter to St. Agnes of Prague: "Farewell in the Lord, and pray for me!" So, too, we may pray for Clare, and Clare prays for us. But most important in this little book, we may pray *with* Clare.

St. Clare's words of prayer can at times be deceptively simple. There are different layers at which most prayers may be used and understood. Scripture works the same way. Drawing on insights from the late Middle Ages, one writer describes the varied ways that we can read the psalms by explaining that the words are "shallow enough for lambs to paddle in [and] deep enough for elephants to swim." Lambs and elephants! Imagine the feet of each animal and the body weight resting on those feet. The same prayer may provide a shallow pool of easy understanding on one occasion, and a deep lake of exploration on another. That is why Clare believed it profits us to pray the same words again and again. Clare's prayers work this way: in other words, they work in more than one way. In the prayer book section of this book we will pray with Clare by focusing on both aspects, the lamb and the elephant. As you pray with Clare, look for the simplicity of her message, but look also for the subtleties and complexities of her understandings of God.

St. Clare's writings are full of Scripture quotes and references. She was drawn to both lamb and elephant passages in the Old and New Testaments. In her prayer life, she would have repeated and ruminated on certain phrases and words over and over again, in her mind and on her lips. She also peppered her writings with Scripture and, in order to understand her prayers more thoroughly, we need to look at those passages that were most dear to her.

PRAYING WITH THE PROPHETS

St. Clare ruminates on and prays often from what are called the wisdom writings of the Hebrew Scriptures, including Song of Solomon, Lamentations, and Proverbs. These books have been a profound source of language for many saints over the ages, particularly in looking for the right words to express love for God, sorrow in the difficulties of life, and disappointment at what seems unfair.

The extended love poem known as Song of Solomon was interpreted allegorically in ancient Judaism as symbolic of the "spousal" love possible between God and human. This method of understanding the Hebrew book of love was adopted by St. Clare and others. Pope Gregory IX alluded to the following passages from Song of Solomon in a letter to Clare and all of the sisters at San Damiano in 1228, two years after St. Francis's death.

> Let him kiss me with the kisses of his mouth!
> For your love is better than wine,
> your anointing oils are fragrant,
> your name is perfume poured out;
> therefore the maidens love you.

> Scarcely had I passed them,
> when I found him whom my soul loves.
> I held him, and would not let him go
> until I brought him into my mother's house,
> and into the chamber of her that conceived me.

But just as she prayed to God at times like a lover, St. Clare also sometimes prayed with the prophet Jeremiah, calling the people of God, who were behaving like adulterers, back to holiness. Loving words of devotion mixed with serious words of challenge in the prayer of Clare. This is one of the ways that her prayers can be like both lambs and elephants.

Lamentations, or the book of Israel's sorrow, was also important to St. Clare's prayers. These two passages from Lamentations stand out as most meaningful in Clare's fourth letter to St. Agnes of Prague:

Is it nothing to you, all you who pass by?
Look and see if there is any sorrow like my
sorrow, which was brought upon me,
which the Lord inflicted on the day of his
fierce anger.

The thought of my affliction and my home-
lessness is wormwood and gall!
My soul continually thinks of it and is bowed
down within me.

PRAYING WITH THE PSALMS

Also from the Old Testament, the Psalms
formed the real backbone of the daily prayers of
St. Clare. They were prayed every day from before
dawn until usually after dusk. Traditionally, on
Fridays, Clare would have prayed Psalm 22, feeling
that she was being crucified along with Christ:
"My God, my God, why have you forsaken me?
and are so far from my cry and from the words
of my distress?"

Psalm 51 was the basis for a daily confession
of one's sins, and it also became the subject of a
dramatic demonstration by St. Francis before the
women of San Damiano: The little poor man was
asked to preach the word of God to the women, and
instead of giving a more traditional address, the
dramatic saint made a circle of ashes, poured

more ashes on his head, and sat down. After a short while, Francis stood and recited the complete psalm as his only sermon.

Sometimes, St. Clare turned to different psalms than St. Francis did. Psalm 45 was particularly meaningful to her:

> Kings' daughters stand among the ladies of
>   the court;
> on your right hand is the queen, adorned
>   with the gold of Ophir.
> "Hear, O daughter; consider and listen closely;
> forget your people and your father's house.
> The king will have pleasure in your beauty;
> he is your master; therefore do him honor.
> The people of Tyre are here with a gift;
> the rich among the people seek your favor."
> All glorious is the princess as she enters;
>   her gown is cloth-of-gold.
> In embroidered apparel she is brought to the
>   king;
> after her the bridesmaids follow in procession.

It is easy to imagine that St. Clare would have viewed her life through the lens of such a psalm. Two years after her death, Thomas of Celano immortalized Clare's life by comparing her time on earth to the words of Psalm 68:13: "you shall be like a dove whose wings are covered with silver, whose feathers are like green gold," adding that that silver dove built a nest in the cleft of the rock that was San Damiano and raised up a community there.

PRAYING WITH THE GOSPELS

Like St. Francis before her, St. Clare was always looking at Jesus' earthly life as her example for what to do and who to become. She read and quoted from the Gospels more than any other Scripture. Also like Francis, Clare quoted most often from Matthew's Gospel out of the canonical four. In the first letter to St. Agnes of Prague, as Clare gives advice on the religious life, she quotes or alludes to Matthew no fewer than ten times. She instructs Agnes to store up treasures in heaven rather than on earth, to love poverty and serve God rather than money, to know the kingdom of heaven by being poor and humble in spirit, and to seek only those treasures that can never be stolen—and those are just the references from Matthew 5 and 6.

St. Clare also appreciated this passage from Matthew 19, where Jesus speaks to Peter saying: "Everyone who has left houses, brothers, sisters, father, mother, children or land for the sake of my name will receive a hundred times as much, and also inherit eternal life." She patterned her life after this teaching, and she instructed others to do likewise.

In addition to Matthew, she prayed frequently with passages from Luke and John but never from Mark. To ask her sisters to own spiritual books only when it was absolutely necessary, St. Clare referenced Luke 9:3, "Take nothing for the journey: neither staff, nor haversack, nor bread, nor money; and do not have a spare tunic." To explain why she often neglected her physical body, she quoted Matthew 6:34, "So do not worry about tomorrow: tomorrow will take care of itself." The Gospels were very dear to Clare and to the life of the Poor Clares.

PRAYING WITH ST. PAUL

Finally, St. Clare reflected in prayer and in her letters on the various letters of St. Paul to the first churches. Both Clare and St. Francis believed that their thirteenth-century spiritual movement was a return to the way of living that marked the earliest Christians. Clare begins her *Testament* by echoing Paul's advice to the first Christians in Corinth: "Consider your own call, brothers and sisters."

Several themes from St. Paul were essential to the prayers of St. Clare. She reflected, for instance, on the premise that a vocation is something never to be concluded; conversion is a lifelong process. Another theme was that the promise of following Christ is an abundant life filled with joy and meaning. In her *Testament*, Clare quoted from the Second Letter of Paul to the Corinthians: "For you know the generous act of our Lord Jesus Christ, that though he was rich, yet for your sakes he became poor, so that by his poverty you might become rich." The Franciscan vocation could be summarized in that one verse.

Morning and Evening Prayer

AN INTRODUCTION

THE FOLLOWING WEEKLY LITURGY is derived from various sources and reflects the concerns of St. Clare of Assisi. Many of the words are the same as those that Clare prayed, and all of them are examples of the spirituality of the first Franciscans. In chapter three of her Rule, Clare urged all of the sisters who could read to celebrate the Divine Office according to the same custom as the Franciscan men. And so, the twice-daily weekly portion of the Divine Office below reflects how Clare may have prayed morning and evening prayer with her sisters, and it also repeats many of the words and phrases that were dear to them.

The sequence for each day of this special morning and evening liturgy is as follows:

A. PREPARATION (a very simple prayer of intention)
B. GOSPEL SENTENCE (the brevity of these passages can be profound, as St. Clare said, like "eating the fruit of a bountiful tree")
C. SILENCE (more than a moment; a minute or more)
D. CONFESSION
E. FIRST READING (a canticle from the Hebrew prophets or New Testament epistles)

F. PSALM

G. GOSPEL READING

H. SILENCE (again)

I. PRAYERS OF THE SAINTS (ones that Clare may
    have prayed or that were written by early
    Franciscans)

J. COLLECT (as Clare may have prayed with her sisters)

There are various ways that you may choose
to use these morning and evening prayers in your
own devotional life. First, they can form a special
prayer book for your daily life as you walk along
with St. Clare and pray the themes that formed
her own spiritual life. If you already have a prayer
book you use daily, you can use this book in
other ways. For example, it can serve as a focus
for your prayer time during a weekend or week-
long spiritual retreat focusing on the life and
message of St. Clare.

The divine hours of prayer have, from their
earliest beginnings in the ancient synagogue, been
intended for group use; therefore, you may wish,
in addition, to pray these short liturgies with others in a group devoted to learning more about
Clare of Assisi. Otherwise, as you pray alone,
know that you are not alone. You join with thousands of Poor Clares around the world both past
and present who have prayed similar words, as
well. For them and for us, daily prayer is a means
of beginning anew each day.

Second, if you already have a prayer practice and a prayer book, this book's offering of a week of special prayers may be a substitute for your regular prayer practice. You may wish to make a special prayer week with St. Clare, finding some fresh inspiration by praying closely with Clare. It is natural to come to these points in any prayer life, which explains the necessity of works such as this one.

Third, while I hope that these prayers become a personal and daily prayer book for many, it may also appeal to those who may wish to pray in community, in study groups of St. Clare, or even in academic settings. There is no way truly to understand the "little plant," as she called herself, without enjoining her spiritual life, themes, and the very words of her prayers.

SEVEN THEMES FOR SEVEN DAYS

Seven themes emerge from the life and writings of St. Clare, and each provides a framework and subject for one of our seven days of prayer.

Day One—Embracing Christ

Quoting Paul's Letter to the Romans, St. Clare wrote in her second letter to St. Agnes of Prague, praising her: "You have offered yourself as a holy and pleasing sacrifice" to God. All Christians are called to do this, whether or not we take a vow of celibacy in a religious life. What could be more true? For Clare, this embrace—or marriage—was total, and it was also Trinitarian. As mentioned above, according to the "Form of Life" written by St. Francis for the sisters, Francis said that the sisters were married to the Holy Spirit. "By divine inspiration you have made yourselves daughters of the most High . . . the heavenly Father, and taken the Holy Spirit as your spouse." The emphasis is on unity with God as Trinity. Elsewhere in the same letter to St. Agnes, Clare describes Francis as an imitator of God the Father. And in her *Testament*, Clare refers to Francis as one who imitated Christ to the point of following his very footprints. All of these ideals of embracing God boil down to seeing oneself entirely in the mirror of Christ, through the aid of the Holy Spirit's leading, and by so doing, to see our true selves.

Day Two—Purity

St. Clare was not pure as if she had put on a gown and clothed herself in righteousness. Following Christ is never that simple, even for saints. Purity was a many-sided pursuit for Clare, and it is an essential aspect of any Christian striving for sanctity in daily life. For Clare, virginal purity was part of her identity, as she followed in the steps of earlier saints such as

St. Agnes of Rome (see the Appendices). But purity has many other sides, both for us and in the prayers of Clare.

Purity is not about being a "young virgin" or going to bed supperless or being "lily white"—as suggested in romantic images from a John Keats poem about St. Agnes—but it is, for St. Clare and for us, about a kind of holiness that happens when we ". . . require / Of Heaven with upward eyes for all that [we] desire."

Sometimes, purity can be quite measurable and straightforward, such as sexual purity. But purity of the heart is different; only God knows how we are doing there. For St. Clare, purity was never a series of negatives: *Thou shalt not. . . .* For Clare, purity was a state of devotedness to God, renewed each day. In purity came single-mindedness, clarity, and freedom.

Day Three—Walking the Path of Conversion

For both St. Francis and St. Clare, the path of conversion was lifelong and daily at the same time. Each of them advocated what today we would call volunteer poverty. In practical terms, they found that simplicity and joy were most essential for life, and neither were to be found in material things. Clare believed that a follower of Christ needs to continually evaluate oneself and strip away those encumbrances that keep one from seeing Christ most clearly. The fewer things one needs, the more liberated one is to become who one is meant to be in Christ.

In chapter six of her Rule, St. Clare preserved St. Francis's final blessing for the sisters, a simple paragraph:

> I, little brother Francis, follow the life and poverty of our most exalted Lord Jesus Christ as well as his most holy Mother, and to persevere in this life until the end. I ask you, my sisters, and I encourage you to live always in this holy life and poverty. Keep careful watch and never depart from it by reason of the contrary teaching of any person.

It was advice full of foreboding, as Francis's movement was torn by those who overturned the founder's commitment to poverty soon after his death. But Clare intended to preserve it for her and her sisters, and she was the guardian of the original Franciscan ideals for the quarter century that she lived after Francis's death.

Day Four—Listening with the Heart

We all live messy lives, and this is usually what causes us to pray. St. Clare leads us through many steps of faith that help us to find our focus once again. So far, we have approached God who embraces us, paid careful attention to the purity of our lives, and focused ourselves on the ongoing path of conversion. Each of these themes serves to bolster our spirits, and deepen our attention, as we pray in the midst of everyday life. Now, we are ready to follow Clare into this fourth stage of listening with the heart.

St. Clare speaks most eloquently on this theme in her third letter to St. Agnes. A heart must always be converted since it naturally leans toward the world. Clare tells Agnes that "the crafty enemy" (which is a combination of the devil and worldly vanity) "infatuates the human heart." But through conversion, we become as Jesus said in the parable, a treasure hidden in a field. The human heart becomes a place of hidden, quiet treasure. God knows its qualities, to be sure, and we gradually do, as well. Such is the process of what theologians call sanctification.

In the second letter to St. Agnes, St. Clare urges her to "gaze, consider, contemplate, and desire" to imitate Jesus. These are very slow activities, and the primary goal of this imitation is to listen for the word of God in our lives. This sort of prayer is not always an activity of the mind, as if we only concentrate ourselves toward God. Sometimes, we listen best for God when we do some simple act of obedience, show love to our neighbor, or carry out a simple task that we know we are supposed to do. This is what Clare means by turning listening into seeing—opening our eyes to what we may not normally see around us—and then into action.

Through all of these activities, we are praying and developing a heart more like Christ's. So, Clare listens with the heart in the same sense that the Apostle Paul understands when he writes to the fledgling church in Philippi: "This is my prayer, that your love may overflow more and more with knowledge and full insight."

Day Five—Adoring Christ

Both St. Francis and St. Clare were visual people; they learned by seeing. Eyes are windows to the soul, and images of Christ can be windows to seeing God. In an icon, when we see Christ, Christ may also see us.

St. Clare also believed that the eyes have a special, spiritual function in the body. For her, looking was akin to touching. Gazing on Christ was the way to see with his eyes, and a way to begin to see our true selves as he sees us.

St. Clare's writings are abundant with metaphors and allusions that show the visual ways that she adored Christ. For example, she wrote, "Happy, indeed, is she to whom it is given to drink at this sacred banquet so that she might cling with her whole heart to Him whose beauty all the blessed hosts of heaven unceasingly admire." This is the language of metaphor and adoration.

She taught her sisters to adore Christ in tangible ways, as well. Prayer, for St. Clare, brought Christ closer. Through the heartfelt words of prayer, we adore Christ in our speech. When we use an icon in prayer, Christ comes closer through our eyes. And caring for the sick and the poor and the stranger (as the Poor Clares often did) was a tangible way of adoring Christ, taking prayer to the next step, following the teaching of Jesus from Matthew 25: "In truth I tell you, in so far as you did this to one of the least of these brothers of mine, you did it to me."

Only a loving, faithful, and creative God would expect such creative responses from human beings in prayer—standards that St. Clare felt to be entirely within the range of possibility in human experience. Like Velveteen rabbits, we become more authentically real the more that we touch, feel, are felt, love, and are loved.

Day Six—True Discipleship

St. Clare thought vividly about Jesus before she ever prayed. Several times Clare repeated the image of following his footprints closely, first mentioned in Scripture. She imagined herself quite literally walking behind Jesus, doing as he did on earth.

For St. Clare, one of the most important ways of being a disciple of Jesus was to pray. Many of Clare's prayers were modeled after the ways that Jesus prayed. At various times and in different ways, Clare spent days and nights in the "desert" in prayer; she went alone in the "garden" to pray; she even wished that her sisters would stay awake more often and pray with her; and she instructed her sisters how to pray the Our Father.

St. Clare measured her faithfulness to Christ, and to St. Francis, through a determined life of prayer. The stories about Clare are full of anecdotes that show her praying the canonical hours in choir, praying while eating, praying while working, and rising in the middle of the night to pray, prompted by the Holy Spirit to do so.

We also know from the tales of St. Francis that he wished nothing more than that the Poor Clares, and St. Clare herself, would illuminate the world with their faithfulness. Clare's name means "light" in Italian, and the image of light surrounds her legend. When Francis and Brother Leo were walking outside at night, it was common for Francis to compare Clare's life of prayer to the brightest stars and to the full moon.

We often consider true discipleship to consist of where we go, what activities we do, and the like, as though we are doing business for the kingdom. But for some Christians, prayer is the primary vocation. And for all of us, a brilliant and devoted life of prayer is a kind of true discipleship that illuminates the world for Christ.

Day Seven—Redefining Family

Both St. Francis and St. Clare turned away from their earthly families in dramatic fashion in order to follow Christ. The drama of those memorable scenes was not accidental. Francis and Clare believed that discipleship with Christ meant making difficult decisions about our lives. We often feel the difficulty of these decisions most acutely when they impact our families. There are times when we must be away from a spouse, children, parents, and other loved ones in order to do what is God's work for us in the world. Francis and Clare wanted to refocus our attention on these ways that the family of God is larger than our own families.

We are not all called to a vowed life, as Sts. Francis and Clare were, but we *are* all called to a life of discipleship. We are called to a life that redefines "family" in ways that Jesus explained two millennia ago.

In Matthew 5, Jesus quotes the Jewish commandments and then adds to them. He modifies an "eye for eye and tooth for tooth" with "Give to anyone who asks you, and if anyone wants to borrow, do not turn away." Jesus tells his followers, "You have heard how it was said, 'You will love your neighbor and hate your enemy.' But I say this to you, love your enemies and pray for those who persecute you; so that you may be children of your Father in heaven."

The saints from Assisi intended to redefine—as Jesus had before them—what it means to be a sister, brother, mother, and father. Just as the Apostle Paul defined true love for the first time in his First Letter to the Corinthians, Jesus defined family and neighbor in ways that had never before been understood. He taught that the prisoner, the outcast, and the unwanted are our brothers and sisters. We should find new ways to show love to them, to show them that they, too, are part of the family of God. St. Francis and St. Clare intended to do nothing less than turn the world upside down. We most often imagine them with birds, and flowers, and rabbits, and calmed wolves by their sides—and living in God's new creation includes these—but we may also pray as prophetic voices with Francis and Clare for the transformation of human relationships.

The Daily Office

FOR SUNDAY THROUGH SATURDAY

MORNING PRAYER
Sunday
(Theme/Intent: Embracing Christ)

PREPARATION

Heavenly Father, we have offered ourselves as a
holy and pleasing sacrifice to you.
Make us mindful of our commitment of our
whole selves
every morning, every noontime, every evening.
Only one thing is necessary and it is you.
Amen.

GOSPEL SENTENCE

OUR LORD, JESUS CHRIST, SAYS: "I am the Way; I
am Truth and Life. No one can come to the
Father except through me. If you know me, you
will know my Father too. From this moment you
know him and have seen him."

—John 14:6–7

SILENCE

CONFESSION
Psalm 51:1–7

Have mercy on me, O God,
  according to your loving-kindness;
in your great compassion blot out my offenses.

Wash me through and through from my wickedness
and cleanse me from my sin.

For I know my transgressions,
and my sin is ever before me.

Against you only have I sinned
and done what is evil in your sight.

And so you are justified when you speak
and upright in your judgment.

Indeed, I have been wicked from my birth,
a sinner from my mother's womb.

For behold, you look for truth deep within me,
and will make me understand wisdom secretly.

My beloved speaks and says to me: "Arise, my love, my fair one, and come away; for now the winter is past, the rain is over and gone. The flowers appear on the earth; the time of singing has come, and the voice of the turtledove is heard in our land. The fig tree puts forth its figs, and the vines are in blossom; they give forth fragrance. Arise, my love, my fair one, and come away."

—Song of Solomon 2:10–13

PSALM 63
Deus, Deus meus

O God, you are my God; eagerly I seek you;
my soul thirsts for you, my flesh faints for you,
as in a barren and dry land where there is no water.

Therefore I have gazed upon you in your holy place,
that I might behold your power and your glory.

For your loving-kindness is better than life itself;
my lips shall give you praise.

So will I bless you as long as I live
and lift up my hands in your Name.

My soul is content, as with marrow and fatness,
and my mouth praises you with joyful lips,

When I remember you upon my bed,
and meditate on you in the night watches.

For you have been my helper,
and under the shadow of your wings I will rejoice.

My soul clings to you;
your right hand holds me fast.

May those who seek my life to destroy it
go down into the depths of the earth;

Let them fall upon the edge of the sword,
and let them be food for jackals.

But the king will rejoice in God;
all those who swear by him will be glad;
for the mouth of those who speak lies shall be
  stopped.

GOSPEL READING

HEAR THE WORD OF THE LORD: Jesus said, "Do not store up treasures for yourselves on earth, where moth and woodworm destroy them and thieves can break in and steal. But store up treasures for yourselves in heaven, where neither moth nor woodworm destroys them and thieves cannot break in and steal. For wherever your treasure is, there will your heart be too. The lamp of the body is the eye. It follows that if your eye is clear, your whole body will be filled with light."

—Matthew 6:19–22

SILENCE

PRAYERS OF THE SAINTS

I would die gladly of love
  if I could.
I have seen clearly with my own eyes
Him whom I love
standing in my soul.
The bride who takes her Lover in—
never needs to go very far.

   —Mechthild of Magdeburg (d. ca. 1282)

Keep Doing What You Are Doing

What you are doing, may you keep on doing
  and do not stop.
But with swiftness, agility, and unswerving feet,
may you go forward with joy and security
knowing that you are on the path of wisdom
  and happiness.
Believe nothing, and agree with nothing

that will turn you away from this commitment.
Nothing should be allowed to prevent you
from offering yourself to the Most High in the
   perfection
to which the Spirit of God has called you.
Amen.   —Clare of Assisi

EVENING PRAYER

Sunday

(Theme/Intent: Embracing Christ)

PREPARATION

O Holy One,
our strength is in you.
May your Holy Spirit
direct and rule our hearts in all ways
today
through Jesus Christ our Lord.
Amen.

GOSPEL SENTENCE

OUR LORD, JESUS CHRIST, SAYS: "I am the bread
of life. No one who comes to me will ever hunger;
no one who believes in me will ever thirst."

—John 6:35

SILENCE

CONFESSION
Psalm 51:1, 8–19

Have mercy on me, O God,
  according to your loving-kindness;
in your great compassion blot out my offenses.

Purge me from my sin, and I shall be pure;
wash me, and I shall be clean indeed.

Make me hear of joy and gladness,
that the body you have broken may rejoice.

Hide your face from my sins
and blot out all my iniquities.

Create in me a clean heart, O God,
and renew a right spirit within me.

Cast me not away from your presence
and take not your holy Spirit from me.

Give me the joy of your saving help again
and sustain me with your bountiful Spirit.

I shall teach your ways to the wicked,
and sinners shall return to you.

Deliver me from death, O God,
   and my tongue shall sing of your righteousness,
O God of my salvation.

Open my lips, O Lord,
and my mouth shall proclaim your praise.

Had you desired it, I would have offered sacrifice,
but you take no delight in burnt-offerings.

The sacrifice of God is a troubled spirit;
a broken and contrite heart, O God, you will not
   despise.

Be favorable and gracious to Zion,
and rebuild the walls of Jerusalem.

FIRST READING

There came a voice from the throne saying:
"Praise our God, all you his servants, you that fear
him, both small and great!" And I heard what
sounded like a vast throng, like the sound of a
mighty torrent or of great peals of thunder, and
they cried: "Hallelujah! The Lord our God, sover-
eign over all, has entered on his reign! Let us
rejoice and shout for joy and pay homage to him,
for the wedding day of the Lamb has come! His
bride has made herself ready, and she has been

given fine linen, shining and clean, to wear." The angel said to me, "Write this: 'Happy are those who are invited to the wedding banquet of the Lamb!'" He added, "These are the very words of God." —Revelation 19:5–9 (REB)

PSALM 134
Ecce nunc

Behold now, bless the LORD,
  all you servants of the LORD,
you that stand by night in the house of the LORD.
Lift up your hands in the holy place and bless the
  LORD;
the LORD who made heaven and earth bless
  you out of Zion.

GOSPEL READING

HEAR THE WORD OF THE LORD: In the beginning was the Word: the Word was with God and the Word was God. He was with God in the beginning. Through him all things came into being, not one thing came into being except through him. What has come into being in him was life, life that was the light of men; and light shines in darkness, and darkness could not overpower it. . . . The Word was the real light that gives light to everyone; he was coming into the world. He was in the world that had come into being through him, and the world did not recognize him. He came to his own and his own people did not accept him. But to those who did accept him he gave power to become children of God, to those who believed in his name who were born not from human stock or human desire or human will but from God himself. The Word became flesh, he lived among us, and we saw his glory.

—John 1:1–5, 9–14a

SILENCE

PRAYERS OF THE SAINTS

Soul of Christ, make me holy,
Body of Christ, be my salvation.
Blood of Christ, let me drink your wine.
Water flowing from the side of Christ, wash me
  clean.
Passion of Christ, strengthen me.
Kind Jesus, hear my prayer;
hide me within your wounds
and keep me close to you.
Defend me from the evil enemy.
Call me at my death
to the fellowship of your saints,
so that I may sing your praise with them
through all eternity. Amen.
—A Prayer to the Redeemer from the Roman Missal

COLLECT

Devote yourself to all that you desire,
the most prized possession above all other things;
that is,
the spirit of the Lord
and the work of God.
Amen.

MORNING PRAYER
Monday

(Theme/Intent: Purity)

PREPARATION

As the saints have turned to you,
again and again, for centuries,
we turn to you today,
again and again.
Our truer self awaits.
Our truer self awaits.

GOSPEL SENTENCE

OUR LORD, JESUS CHRIST, SAYS: "The kingdom of
Heaven is like treasure hidden in a field which
someone has found; he hides it again, goes off in his
joy, sells everything he owns and and buys the field.
Again, the kingdom of Heaven is like a merchant
looking for fine pearls; when he finds one of great
value he goes and sells everything he owns and
buys it."   —Matthew 13:44–46

SILENCE

Have mercy on me, O God,
  according to your loving-kindness;
in your great compassion blot out my offenses.

Wash me through and through from my wickedness
and cleanse me from my sin.

For I know my transgressions,
and my sin is ever before me.

Against you only have I sinned
and done what is evil in your sight.

And so you are justified when you speak
and upright in your judgment.

Indeed, I have been wicked from my birth,
a sinner from my mother's womb.

For behold, you look for truth deep within me,
and will make me understand wisdom secretly.

FIRST READING

I appeal to you therefore, brothers and sisters, by
the mercies of God, to present your bodies as a

living sacrifice, holy and acceptable to God, which is your spiritual worship. Do not be conformed to this world, but be transformed by the renewing of your minds, so that you may discern what is the will of God—what is good and acceptable and perfect. . . . Let love be genuine; hate what is evil, hold fast to what is good; love one another with mutual affection; outdo one another in showing honor. Do not lag in zeal, be ardent in spirit, serve the Lord. Rejoice in hope, be patient in suffering, persevere in prayer.

—Romans 12:1–2, 9–12

Psalm 31:19–24

How great is your goodness, O LORD!
which you have laid up for those who fear you;
which you have done in the sight of all
for those who put their trust in you.

You hide them in the covert of your presence
    from those
who slander them;
you keep them in your shelter from the strife of
    tongues.

Blessed be the LORD!
for he has shown me the wonders of his love in a
besieged city.

Yet I said in my alarm,
"I have been cut off from the sight of your eyes."
Nevertheless, you heard the sound of my entreaty
when I cried out to you.

Love the LORD, all you who worship him;
the LORD protects the faithful,
but repays to the full those who act haughtily.

Be strong and let your heart take courage,
all you who wait for the LORD.

GOSPEL READING

HEAR THE WORD OF THE LORD: Jesus told them [a] parable but they failed to understand what he was saying to them. So Jesus spoke to them again: "In all truth I tell you, I am the gate of the sheepfold. All who have come before me are thieves and bandits, but the sheep took no notice of them. I am the gate. Anyone who enters through me will be safe: such a one will go in and out and will find pasture. The thief comes only to steal and kill and destroy. I have come so that they may have life and have it to the full. I am the good shepherd: the good shepherd lays down his life for his sheep. . . .

"I am the good shepherd; I know my own and my own know me, just as the Father knows me and I know the Father; and I lay down my life for my sheep. And there are other sheep I have that are not of this fold, and I must lead these too. They too will listen to my voice, and there will be only one flock, one shepherd."

—John 10:6–11, 14–16

SILENCE

PRAYERS OF THE SAINTS

Fear not, my daughter, He told me,
I am medicine that heals all, heart and soul.
The sins of your eyes, which looked at vain and
    hurtful things, and delighted in things other
    than God.
Your ears, which listened to slander, insults, lies
    and blasphemies.
Your tongue, which ran on about the same.
Your mouth and throat, which delighted too
    much in food and drink.
Your neck, which you have held with anger and
    pride.
Your hands, that have touched and embraced
    many things that you shouldn't have.
And your heart, too often sad, covetous, and
    angry.
Fear not, my daughter, He told me,
I am medicine that heals all, heart and soul.

—Blessed Angela of Foligno (d. 1309)

TRADITIONAL COLLECT
FOR THE FEAST OF ST. AGNES

Almighty, eternal God,
You choose what the world considers weak
to put the worldly power to shame.
May we who celebrate the birth of Saint Agnes
   into eternal joy
be loyal to the faith she professed.
Grant this through our Lord Jesus Christ, Your Son,
who lives and reigns with You and the Holy
   Spirit,
one God, for ever and ever.
Amen.

EVENING PRAYER
Monday
(Theme/Intent: Purity)

PREPARATION

Now, remember: It is God
who set you apart
before you were born,
calling your name,
revealing his Son to you,
so that you might say it again
to every human being.

GOSPEL SENTENCE

OUR LORD, JESUS CHRIST, SAYS: "Your light must
shine in people's sight, so that, seeing your good
works, they may give praise to your Father in
heaven." —Matthew 5:16

SILENCE

Psalm 51:1, 8–19

Have mercy on me, O God, according to your
   loving-kindness;
in your great compassion blot out my offenses.

Purge me from my sin, and I shall be pure;
wash me, and I shall be clean indeed.

Make me hear of joy and gladness,
that the body you have broken may rejoice.

Hide your face from my sins
and blot out all my iniquities.

Create in me a clean heart, O God,
and renew a right spirit within me.

Cast me not away from your presence
and take not your holy Spirit from me.

Give me the joy of your saving help again
and sustain me with your bountiful Spirit.

I shall teach your ways to the wicked,
and sinners shall return to you.

Deliver me from death, O God,
   and my tongue shall sing of your righteousness,
O God of my salvation.

Open my lips, O Lord,
and my mouth shall proclaim your praise.

Had you desired it, I would have offered sacrifice,
but you take no delight in burnt-offerings.

The sacrifice of God is a troubled spirit;
a broken and contrite heart, O God, you will not
   despise.

Be favorable and gracious to Zion,
and rebuild the walls of Jerusalem.

FIRST READING

The Canticle of the Three Young Men
Let the earth bless the Lord:
   praise and glorify him for ever!
Bless the Lord, mountains and hills,
   praise and glorify him for ever!
Bless the Lord, every plant that grows,
   praise and glorify him for ever!
Bless the Lord, springs of water,
   praise and glorify him for ever!
Bless the Lord, seas and rivers,
   praise and glorify him for ever!

Bless the Lord, whales, and everything that moves
  in the waters, praise and glorify him for ever!
Bless the Lord, every kind of bird,
  praise and glorify him for ever!
Bless the Lord, all animals wild and tame,
  praise and glorify him for ever!
Bless the Lord, all the human race:
  praise and glorify him for ever!
Bless the Lord, O Israel,
  praise and glorify him for ever!
Bless the Lord, priests,
  praise and glorify him for ever!
Bless the Lord, his servants,
  praise and glorify him for ever!
Bless the Lord, spirits and souls of the upright,
  praise and glorify him for ever!
Bless the Lord, faithful, humble-hearted people,
  praise and glorify him for ever!
                    —Daniel 3:74–87 (NJB)

PSALM 23
Dominus regit me

The LORD is my shepherd;
I shall not be in want.

He makes me lie down in green pastures
and leads me beside still waters.

He revives my soul
and guides me along right pathways for his
   Name's sake.

Though I walk through the valley of the shadow
   of death,
I shall fear no evil;
for you are with me;
your rod and your staff, they comfort me.

You spread a table before me in the presence of
   those
who trouble me;
you have anointed my head with oil,
and my cup is running over.

Surely your goodness and mercy shall follow me
all the days of my life,
and I will dwell in the house of the LORD for ever.

GOSPEL READING

HEAR THE WORD OF THE LORD: Jesus said, "Pay attention to the parable of the sower. When anyone hears the word of the kingdom without understanding, the Evil One comes and carries off what was sown in his heart: this is the seed sown on the edge of the path. The seed sown on patches of rock is someone who hears the word and welcomes it at once with joy. But such a person has no root deep down and does not last; should some trial come, or some persecution on account of the word, at once he falls away. The seed sown in thorns is someone who hears the word, but the worry of the world and the lure of riches choke the word and so it produces nothing. And the seed sown in rich soil is someone who hears the word and understands it; this is the one who yields a harvest."

—Matthew 13:18–23a

SILENCE

PRAYERS OF THE SAINTS

Eternal God, on you I have depended since my mother's womb; you my soul has loved with all of its strength, and to you I dedicated my body and my soul from childhood. Remember me in your kingdom, for I have been crucified with you. Do not let the abyss of death separate me from your chosen ones, and do not allow the accuser to stand in my way. Forgive me all of my sins so that my soul may be received in your sight, blameless as your Son. Amen.

—St. Macrina the Younger (d. 379)

A COLLECT FOR THE LADIES OF SAN DAMIANO

Live always in truth,
    so that you may die in obedience.
Do not look longingly at life lived outside,
    for the Spirit is better.
In love, use discernment,
    and all that the Lord gives you.
When weighed down by illness, or wearied:
    bear it all in peace and contentment.
For you will one day sell all weariness at a high
    price and you will be crowned a queen in heaven
    with the Virgin Mary. Amen.

                        —St. Francis of Assisi

MORNING PRAYER
Tuesday
(Theme/Intent:
Walking the Path of Conversion)

PREPARATION

As the deer longs for the water-brooks,
so longs my soul for you, O God.
—Psalm 42:1

GOSPEL SENTENCE
Our Lord, Jesus Christ, says: "For wherever your
treasure is, that is where your heart will be too."
—Luke 12:34

SILENCE

CONFESSION
Psalm 51:1–7

Have mercy on me, O God,
according to your loving-kindness;
in your great compassion blot out my offenses.

Wash me through and through from my wickedness
and cleanse me from my sin.

For I know my transgressions,
and my sin is ever before me.

Against you only have I sinned
and done what is evil in your sight.

And so you are justified when you speak
and upright in your judgment.

Indeed, I have been wicked from my birth,
a sinner from my mother's womb.

For behold, you look for truth deep within me,
and will make me understand wisdom secretly.

FIRST READING

Now the Lord is the Spirit, and where the Spirit
of the Lord is, there is freedom. And all of us,
with unveiled faces, seeing the glory of the Lord
as though reflected in a mirror, are being transformed into the same image from one degree of
glory to another; for this comes from the Lord,
the Spirit.

—2 Corinthians 3:17–18

PSALM 119:1–8
Beati immaculati

Happy are they whose way is blameless,
who walk in the law of the LORD!

Happy are they who observe his decrees
and seek him with all their hearts!

Who never do any wrong,
but always walk in his ways.

You laid down your commandments,
that we should fully keep them.

Oh, that my ways were made so direct
that I might keep your statutes!

Then I should not be put to shame,
when I regard all your commandments.

I will thank you with an unfeigned heart,
when I have learned your righteous judgments.

I will keep your statutes;
do not utterly forsake me.

GOSPEL READING

HEAR THE WORD OF THE LORD: Jesus said, "Why do you call me, 'Lord, Lord' and not do what I say? Everyone who comes to me and listens to my words and acts on them—I will show you what such a person is like. Such a person is like the man who, when he built a house, dug, and dug deep, and laid the foundations on rock; when the river was in flood it bore down on that house but could not shake it, it was so well built. But someone who listens and does nothing is like the man who built a house on soil, with no foundations; as soon as the river bore down on it, it collapsed; and what a ruin that house became!"

—Luke 6:46–49

SILENCE

PRAYERS OF THE SAINTS

Lord and protector, you are our redemption. Direct our minds by your gracious presence, and watch over our paths with guiding love; so that, among the snares that lie hidden in the path where we walk, we may pass onward with hearts fixed on you; so that by the track of faith we may come to be where you would have us to be. Amen.

—Mozarabic Sacramentary

COLLECT

May the Lord make you a gardener
among the vines,
pulling weeds, aerating soil,
tending to the needs of both the roots and leaves.
The vines will flourish and grow,
giving forth their fragrance,
spreading their bounty in the light.
May it be so. Amen.

EVENING PRAYER
Tuesday
(Theme/Intent:
Walking the Path of Conversion)

PREPARATION

Author of eternal light,
shed continual day on we who watch for you,
so that our lips may praise you,
our lives may bless you, and
our meditations may glorify you,
through Christ our Lord. Amen.
—Sarum Breviary

GOSPEL SENTENCE

OUR LORD, JESUS CHRIST, SAYS: "You are salt for
the earth. But if salt loses its taste, what can make
it salty again? . . . You are light for the world. A
city built on a hill-top cannot be hidden."

—Matthew 5:13a, 14

SILENCE

CONFESSION
Psalm 51:1, 8–19

Have mercy on me, O God,
   according to your loving-kindness;
in your great compassion blot out my offenses.

Purge me from my sin, and I shall be pure;
wash me, and I shall be clean indeed.

Make me hear of joy and gladness,
that the body you have broken may rejoice.

Hide your face from my sins
and blot out all my iniquities.

Create in me a clean heart, O God,
and renew a right spirit within me.

Cast me not away from your presence
and take not your holy Spirit from me.

Give me the joy of your saving help again
and sustain me with your bountiful Spirit.

I shall teach your ways to the wicked,
and sinners shall return to you.

Deliver me from death, O God,
    and my tongue shall sing of your righteousness,
O God of my salvation.

Open my lips, O Lord,
and my mouth shall proclaim your praise.

Had you desired it, I would have offered sacrifice,
but you take no delight in burnt-offerings.

The sacrifice of God is a troubled spirit;
a broken and contrite heart, O God, you will not
    despise.

Be favorable and gracious to Zion,
and rebuild the walls of Jerusalem.

FIRST READING

May you be made strong with all the strength that
comes from his glorious power, and may you be
prepared to endure everything with patience,
while joyfully giving thanks to the Father, who
has enabled you to share in the inheritance of the
saints in the light. He has rescued us from the
power of darkness and transferred us into the
kingdom of his beloved Son, in whom we have
redemption, the forgiveness of sins. He is the image
of the invisible God, the firstborn of all creation;
for in him all things in heaven and on earth were

created, things visible and invisible, whether thrones or dominions or rulers or powers—all things have been created through him and for him. He himself is before all things, and in him all things hold together.

—Colossians 1:11–17

PSALM 131
Domine, non est

O LORD, I am not proud;
I have no haughty looks.

I do not occupy myself with great matters,
or with things that are too hard for me.

But I still my soul and make it quiet,
like a child upon its mother's breast;
   my soul is quieted within me.

O Israel, wait upon the LORD,
from this time forth for evermore.

HEAR THE WORD OF THE LORD: Jesus took with him Peter and James and his brother John and led them up a high mountain by themselves. There in their presence he was transfigured: his face shone like the sun and his clothes became as dazzling as light. And suddenly Moses and Elijah appeared to them; they were talking with him. Then Peter spoke to Jesus. "Lord," he said, "it is wonderful for us to be here; if you want me to, I will make three shelters here, one for you, one for Moses and one for Elijah." He was still speaking when suddenly a bright cloud covered them with shadow, and suddenly from the cloud there came a voice which said, "This is my Son, the Beloved; he enjoys my favor. Listen to him." When they heard this, the disciples fell on their faces, overcome with fear. But Jesus came up and touched them, saying, "Stand up, do not be afraid." And when they raised their eyes they saw no one but Jesus.

—Matthew 17:1–8

SILENCE

PRAYERS OF THE SAINTS

Let us rise up without delay! The scriptures challenge us with these words: "You know what time it is, how it is now the moment for you to wake from sleep." Let us open our eyes to the light that transfigures everything; let us clear our ears for the sound of God's voice that cries out to us each day: "Oh, that today you would hearken to his voice! Harden not your hearts."

—St. Benedict of Nursia (d. 550)

COLLECT

May you have tremendous joy, obtaining the one thing worth desiring,
but remain surprised by God, with awe for God's gift in you.
Be an essential co-worker in the heavenly field, a co-creator in the work of God,
a support for the Body of Christ. Amen.

MORNING PRAYER
Wednesday

(Theme/Intent: Listening with the Heart)

PREPARATION

Almighty God, unto whom all hearts are open,
all desires known, and from whom no secrets
are hid: cleanse the thoughts of our hearts by
the inspiration of your Holy Spirit, that we
may perfectly love you, and worthily magnify
your holy name, through Jesus Christ our Lord.
Amen.

—Gregorian Sacramentary

GOSPEL SENTENCE

OUR LORD, JESUS CHRIST, SAYS: "Whoever holds
to my commandments and keeps them is the one
who loves me; and whoever loves me will be loved
by my Father, and I shall love him and reveal
myself to him."   —John 14:21

SILENCE

Have mercy on me, O God,
   according to your loving-kindness;
in your great compassion blot out my offenses.

Wash me through and through from my wickedness
and cleanse me from my sin.

For I know my transgressions,
and my sin is ever before me.

Against you only have I sinned
and done what is evil in your sight.

And so you are justified when you speak
and upright in your judgment.

Indeed, I have been wicked from my birth,
a sinner from my mother's womb.

For behold, you look for truth deep within me,
and will make me understand wisdom secretly.

FIRST READING

Now the Lord is the Spirit, and where the Spirit
of the Lord is, there is freedom. And all of us,
with unveiled faces, seeing the glory of the Lord as

though reflected in a mirror, are being transformed
into the same image from one degree of glory to
another; for this comes from the Lord, the Spirit.
—2 Corinthians 3:17–18

PSALM 119:17–32
Retribue servo tuo

Deal bountifully with your servant,
that I may live and keep your word.

Open my eyes, that I may see
the wonders of your law.

I am a stranger here on earth;
do not hide your commandments from me.

My soul is consumed at all times
with longing for your judgments.

You have rebuked the insolent;
cursed are they who stray from your
    commandments!

Turn from me shame and rebuke,
for I have kept your decrees.

Even though rulers sit and plot against me,
I will meditate on your statutes.

For your decrees are my delight,
and they are my counselors.

My soul cleaves to the dust;
give me life according to your word.

I have confessed my ways, and you answered me;
instruct me in your statutes.

Make me understand the way of your commandments,
that I may meditate on your marvelous works.

My soul melts away for sorrow;
strengthen me according to your word.

Take from me the way of lying;
let me find grace through your law.

I have chosen the way of faithfulness;
I have set your judgments before me.

I hold fast to your decrees;
O LORD, let me not be put to shame.

I will run the way of your commandments,
for you have set my heart at liberty.

GOSPEL READING

HEAR THE WORD OF THE LORD: Jesus said, "The sheep that belong to me listen to my voice; I know them and they follow me. I give them eternal life; they will never be lost and no one will ever steal them from my hand. The Father, for what he has given me, is greater than anyone, and no one can steal anything from the Father's hand."

—John 10:27–29

SILENCE

PRAYERS OF THE SAINTS

O God, in whom is the well of life, and
in whose light we may see light:
increase in us, we ask, the shine of divine knowledge,
that we may reach your fountain.
Impart to our thirsting souls the drink of life, and
restore to our darkened minds the light of heaven.

—Mozarabic Sacramentary

COLLECT

May Holy Wisdom
rise like a fine mist among you.
She is the radiance that reflects
eternal light,
and a mirror of the working of God.
She is one,
and makes all things new,
entering holy souls
making them the friends of God. Amen.

EVENING PRAYER
Wednesday

(Theme/Intent:Listening with the Heart)

PREPARATION

For God alone my soul in silence waits;
from him comes my salvation.
—Psalm 62:1

GOSPEL SENTENCE

OUR LORD, JESUS CHRIST, SAYS: "Blessed are
those who have not seen and yet believe."
—John 20:29

SILENCE

CONFESSION
Psalm 51:1, 8–19

Have mercy on me, O God,
according to your loving-kindness;
in your great compassion blot out my offenses.

Purge me from my sin, and I shall be pure;
wash me, and I shall be clean indeed.

Make me hear of joy and gladness,
that the body you have broken may rejoice.

Hide your face from my sins
and blot out all my iniquities.

Create in me a clean heart, O God,
and renew a right spirit within me.

Cast me not away from your presence
and take not your holy Spirit from me.

Give me the joy of your saving help again
and sustain me with your bountiful Spirit.

I shall teach your ways to the wicked,
and sinners shall return to you.

Deliver me from death, O God,
  and my tongue shall sing of your righteousness,
O God of my salvation.

Open my lips, O Lord,
and my mouth shall proclaim your praise.

Had you desired it, I would have offered sacrifice,
but you take no delight in burnt-offerings.

The sacrifice of God is a troubled spirit;
a broken and contrite heart, O God, you will not
   despise.

Be favorable and gracious to Zion,
and rebuild the walls of Jerusalem.

FIRST READING

Hear the word of the LORD, O nations, and
declare it in the coastlands far away; say, "He who
scattered Israel will gather him, and will keep him
as a shepherd a flock." For the LORD has ran-
somed Jacob, and has redeemed him from hands
too strong for him. They shall come and sing
aloud on the height of Zion, and they shall be
radiant over the goodness of the LORD, over the
grain, the wine, and the oil, and over the young
of the flock and the herd; their life shall become
like a watered garden, and they shall never languish again. Then shall the young women rejoice
in the dance, and the young men and the old shall
be merry. I will turn their mourning into joy, I
will comfort them, and give them gladness for
sorrow. I will give the priests their fill of fatness,
and my people shall be satisfied with my bounty,
says the LORD.

—Jeremiah 31:10–14

PSALM 42:1–7
Quemadmodum

As the deer longs for the water-brooks,
so longs my soul for you, O God.

My soul is athirst for God, athirst for the living God;
when shall I come to appear before the presence
   of God?

My tears have been my food day and night,
while all day long they say to me,
   "Where now is your God?"

I pour out my soul when I think on these things:
how I went with the multitude and led them into
   the house of God,

With the voice of praise and thanksgiving,
among those who keep holy-day.

Why are you so full of heaviness, O my soul?
and why are you so disquieted within me?

Put your trust in God;
for I will yet give thanks to him,
   who is the help of my countenance, and my
   God.

GOSPEL READING

HEAR THE WORD OF THE LORD: Jesus said, "I say to you: Ask, and it will be given to you; search, and you will find; knock, and the door will be opened to you. For everyone who asks receives; everyone who searches finds; everyone who knocks will have the door opened. What father among you, if his son asked for a fish, would hand him a snake? Or if he asked for an egg, hand him a scorpion? If you then, evil as you are, know how to give your children what is good, how much more will the heavenly Father give the Holy Spirit to those who ask him!"

—Luke 11:9–13

SILENCE

PRAYERS OF THE SAINTS

I would like the angels of Heaven to be among us. I would like an abundance of peace. I would like vessels full of charity and rich treasures of mercy. I would like cheerfulness to preside over all people, and I would like Jesus to be present. I would like the three Marys of illustrious renown to be with us, and I would like the friends of Heaven to be gathered around us from all over and forever. Amen.   —St. Brigid (d. 525)

COLLECT

Now, in the name of God,
who chose you and set you apart
from the time when you were in
your mother's womb, and by His grace
revealed his Son to you:
Preach with your lives,
and when necessary,
use words.
Amen.

Thursday

PREPARATION

I bend my knee
to the Father of our Lord Jesus Christ.
Through the prayers of our glorious
Virgin Mary, Christ's holy mother,
and of our blessed father Francis
and all of the saints,
may the Lord who has given us
such a good beginning
increase the gift and the blessing
and our final perseverance together.
Amen.
—Clare of Assisi

GOSPEL SENTENCE

OUR LORD, JESUS CHRIST, SAYS: "How blessed are the poor in spirit: the kingdom of Heaven is theirs. . . . Blessed are the pure in heart: they shall see God." —Matthew 5:3, 8

CONFESSION
Psalm 51:1–7

Have mercy on me, O God,
  according to your loving-kindness;
in your great compassion blot out my offenses.

Wash me through and through from my wickedness
and cleanse me from my sin.

For I know my transgressions,
and my sin is ever before me.

Against you only have I sinned
and done what is evil in your sight.

And so you are justified when you speak
and upright in your judgment.

Indeed, I have been wicked from my birth,
a sinner from my mother's womb.

For behold, you look for truth deep within me,
and will make me understand wisdom secretly.

FIRST READING

Of this gospel I have become a servant according
to the gift of God's grace that was given me by the

working of his power. . . . For this reason I bow my knees before the Father, from whom every family in heaven and on earth takes its name. I pray that, according to the riches of his glory, he may grant that you may be strengthened in your inner being with power through his Spirit, and that Christ may dwell in your hearts through faith, as you are being rooted and grounded in love. I pray that you may have the power to comprehend, with all the saints, what is the breadth and length and height and depth, and to know the love of Christ that surpasses knowledge, so that you may be filled with all the fullness of God.

—Ephesians 3:7, 14–19

Psalm 51:10–12, 15-17

Hide your face from my sins
and blot out all my iniquities.

Create in me a clean heart, O God,
and renew a right spirit within me.

Cast me not away from your presence
and take not your holy Spirit from me.

Deliver me from death, O God,
and my tongue shall sing of your righteousness,
    O God of my salvation.

Open my lips, O Lord,
and my mouth shall proclaim your praise.

Had you desired it, I would have offered sacrifice,
but you take no delight in burnt-offerings.

HEAR THE WORD OF THE LORD: Now as they went on their way, he entered a certain village, where a woman named Martha welcomed him into her home. She had a sister named Mary, who sat at the Lord's feet and listened to what he was saying. But Martha was distracted by her many tasks; so she came to him and asked, "Lord, do you not care that my sister has left me to do all the work by myself? Tell her then to help me." But the Lord answered her, "Martha, Martha, you are worried and distracted by many things; there is need of only one thing. Mary has chosen the better part."

—Luke 10:38–42a (NRSV)

SILENCE

PRAYERS OF THE SAINTS

Pierce my soul, sweet Lord Jesus, with the most joyous and wholesome wound of your love, and with calm, true, and holy love. Make my soul to languish and melt with love and longing for you, yearn for you and for your courts, longing to be dissolved with you. May my heart always hunger after and feed on you. May it always thirst for you, the fountain of life, of all wisdom and knowledge, of eternal light, a torrent of pleasure, the house of God. You alone will be my hope, my confidence, riches, delight, pleasure, joy, rest, peace, sweetness, food, luxury, refuge, help, wisdom, and treasure. In you will my soul and heart ever be fixed and firm, immovable. Amen.

—St. Bonaventure (d. 1274)

COLLECT

Holy One,
fill us with reverence and joy,
as our spirit withdraws
little by little
from what is worldly to a more fiery longing for God.
And may we turn away from the fleeting things
that keep us from drawing near
to the solid land of prayer.

EVENING PRAYER
Thursday

(Theme/Intent: Adoring Christ)

PREPARATION

Incline your merciful ears, Lord,
and illuminate the darkness of our hearts
by the light
of your visitation.
Amen.
—Gelasian Sacramentary

GOSPEL SENTENCE

OUR LORD, JESUS CHRIST, SAYS: "God is spirit, and those who worship must worship in spirit and truth."   —John 4:24

SILENCE

CONFESSION
Psalm 51:1, 8–19

Have mercy on me, O God,
   according to your loving-kindness;
in your great compassion blot out my offenses.

Purge me from my sin, and I shall be pure;
wash me, and I shall be clean indeed.

Make me hear of joy and gladness,
   that the body you have broken may rejoice.

Hide your face from my sins
and blot out all my iniquities.

Create in me a clean heart, O God,
and renew a right spirit within me.

Cast me not away from your presence
and take not your holy Spirit from me.

Give me the joy of your saving help again
and sustain me with your bountiful Spirit.

I shall teach your ways to the wicked,
and sinners shall return to you.

Deliver me from death, O God,
   and my tongue shall sing of your righteousness,
O God of my salvation.

Open my lips, O Lord,
and my mouth shall proclaim your praise.

Had you desired it, I would have offered sacrifice,
but you take no delight in burnt-offerings.

The sacrifice of God is a troubled spirit;
a broken and contrite heart, O God, you will not
  despise.

Be favorable and gracious to Zion,
and rebuild the walls of Jerusalem.

FIRST READING

For wisdom is more mobile than any motion;
because of her pureness she pervades and penetrates
all things. For she is a breath of the power of God,
and a pure emanation of the glory of the
Almighty; therefore nothing defiled gains
entrance into her. For she is a reflection of eternal
light, a spotless mirror of the working of God,
and an image of his goodness.

—Wisdom of Solomon 7:24–26

PSALM 16:1–2, 5–11
Conserva me, Domine

Protect me, O God, for I take refuge in you;
I have said to the LORD, "You are my Lord,
my good above all other."

All my delight is upon the godly that are in the land,
upon those who are noble among the people.

O LORD, you are my portion and my cup;
it is you who uphold my lot.

My boundaries enclose a pleasant land;
indeed, I have a goodly heritage.

I will bless the LORD who gives me counsel;
my heart teaches me, night after night.

I have set the LORD always before me;
because he is at my right hand I shall not fall.

My heart, therefore, is glad, and my spirit rejoices;
my body also shall rest in hope.

For you will not abandon me to the grave,
nor let your holy one see the Pit.

You will show me the path of life;
in your presence there is fullness of joy,
   and in your right hand are pleasures
   for evermore.

GOSPEL READING

HEAR THE WORD OF THE LORD: Jesus said, "Do
not let your hearts be troubled. You trust in God,

trust also in me. In my Father's house there are many places to live in; otherwise I would have told you. I am going now to prepare a place for you, and after I have gone and prepared you a place, I shall return to take you to myself, so that you may be with me where I am. You know the way to the place where I am going."   —John 14:1–4

SILENCE

PRAYERS OF THE SAINTS

I adore, I venerate, I glory in the holy cross, and in our merciful Lord and what he has done for us. By you, hell is spoiled; its mouth is closed to the redeemed. By you, demons are afraid, restrained, and defeated. By you, the whole world is renewed and made beautiful.

—St. Anselm (d. 1109)

COLLECT

O God,
unworthy servants of Christ as we are,
may we sing a new song
in the midst of your holy presence
before your very throne,
and follow the Lamb of God
wherever he goes.
Amen.

MORNING PRAYER
Friday

(Theme/Intent: True Discipleship)

PREPARATION

Most loving God,
you set me apart before I was born
and called me through grace.
You revealed your blessed Son to me,
so that I might bless you.

GOSPEL SENTENCE

OUR LORD, JESUS CHRIST, SAYS: "No one can be
the slave of two masters: he will either hate the
first and love the second, or be attached to the
first and despise the second."   —Matthew 6:24a

SILENCE

CONFESSION
Psalm 51:1–7

Have mercy on me, O God,
   according to your loving-kindness;
in your great compassion blot out my offenses.

Wash me through and through from my wickedness
and cleanse me from my sin.

For I know my transgressions,
and my sin is ever before me.

Against you only have I sinned
and done what is evil in your sight.

And so you are justified when you speak
and upright in your judgment.

Indeed, I have been wicked from my birth,
a sinner from my mother's womb.

For behold, you look for truth deep within me,
and will make me understand wisdom secretly.

FIRST READING

Let the same mind be in you that was in Christ
Jesus, who, though he was in the form of God,
did not regard equality with God as something to
be exploited, but emptied himself, taking the

form of a slave, being born in human likeness. And being found in human form, he humbled himself and became obedient to the point of death—even death on a cross. Therefore God also highly exalted him and gave him the name that is above every name, so that at the name of Jesus every knee should bend, in heaven and on earth and under the earth, and every tongue should confess that Jesus Christ is Lord, to the glory of God the Father.

—Philippians 2:5–11

PSALM 50:1–6, 14–15
Deus deorum

The LORD, the God of gods, has spoken;
he has called the earth from the rising of the sun
 to its setting.

Out of Zion, perfect in its beauty,
God reveals himself in glory.

Our God will come and will not keep silence;
before him there is a consuming flame,
 and round about him a raging storm.

He calls the heavens and the earth from above
to witness the judgment of his people.

"Gather before me my loyal followers,
those who have made a covenant with me
and sealed it with sacrifice."

Let the heavens declare the rightness of his cause;
for God himself is judge.

"Offer to God a sacrifice of thanksgiving
and make good your vows to the Most High.

Call upon me in the day of trouble;
I will deliver you, and you shall honor me."

GOSPEL READING

HEAR THE WORD OF THE LORD: When Jesus saw the crowd all about him he gave orders to leave for the other side. One of the scribes then came up and said to him, "Master, I will follow you wherever you go." Jesus said, "Foxes have holes and the birds of the air have nests, but the Son of man has nowhere to lay his head." Another man, one of the disciples, said to him, "Lord, let me go and bury my father first." But Jesus said, "Follow me, and leave the dead to bury their dead." Then he got into the boat, followed by his disciples. Suddenly a storm broke over the lake, so violent that the boat was being swamped by the waves. But he was asleep. So they went to him and woke him, saying, "Save us, Lord, we are lost!" And he said to them, "Why are you so frightened, you who have so little faith?" And then he stood up and rebuked the winds and the sea; and there was a great calm. They were astounded and said, "Whatever kind of man is this, that even the winds and the sea obey him?"

—Matthew 8:18–27

SILENCE

PRAYERS OF THE SAINTS

"Make Your Prayer Like a Mother"
A prayer is surely a mother when it conceives virtues by the love of God, and brings them forth in the love of neighbors. Where do you show love, faith, hope, and humility? In prayer.

Mental prayer is the motherhood of prayer. By mental prayer the soul receives the reward for the labors she underwent in her imperfect vocal prayer. Then she tastes the milk of faithful prayer. She rises above herself—that is, above the gross impulse of the senses—and with angelic mind unites herself with God by force of love, and sees and knows with the light of thought, clothing herself with truth.

—St. Catherine of Siena (d. 1380)

COLLECT

Give strength, O Lord, to those who see you,
and continually pour into their souls the
holy desire of seeking you;
that they who long to see your face may not crave
the world's pernicious pleasure.
Amen.

—Mozarabic Sacramentary

EVENING PRAYER
Friday

(Theme/Intent: True Discipleship)

PREPARATION

You are the Holy One,
image of the invisible God;
before all things,
and in whom all things hold together.
Amen.

GOSPEL SENTENCE

OUR LORD, JESUS CHRIST, SAYS: "Enter by the narrow gate, since the road that leads to destruction is wide and spacious, and many take it; but it is a narrow gate and a hard road that leads to life, and only a few find it."

—Matthew 7:13–14

SILENCE

CONFESSION
Psalm 51:1, 8–19

Have mercy on me, O God,
   according to your loving-kindness;
in your great compassion blot out my offenses.

Purge me from my sin, and I shall be pure;
wash me, and I shall be clean indeed.

Make me hear of joy and gladness,
that the body you have broken may rejoice.

Hide your face from my sins
and blot out all my iniquities.

Create in me a clean heart, O God,
and renew a right spirit within me.

Cast me not away from your presence
and take not your holy Spirit from me.

Give me the joy of your saving help again
and sustain me with your bountiful Spirit.

I shall teach your ways to the wicked,
and sinners shall return to you.

Deliver me from death, O God,
and my tongue shall sing of your righteousness,
   O God of my salvation.

Open my lips, O Lord,
and my mouth shall proclaim your praise.

Had you desired it, I would have offered sacrifice,
but you take no delight in burnt-offerings.

The sacrifice of God is a troubled spirit;
a broken and contrite heart, O God, you will not
    despise.

Be favorable and gracious to Zion,
and rebuild the walls of Jerusalem.

FIRST READING

I shall take you from among the nations, and
gather you from every land, and bring you to
your homeland. I shall sprinkle pure water over
you, and you will be purified from everything
that defiles you; I shall purify you from the taint
of all your idols. I shall give you a new heart and
put a new spirit within you; I shall remove the
heart of stone from your body and give you a
heart of flesh.

—Ezekiel 36:24–26 (REB)

PSALM 46
Deus noster refugium

God is our refuge and strength,
a very present help in trouble.

Therefore we will not fear, though the earth be
    moved,
and though the mountains be toppled into the
    depths of the sea;

Though its waters rage and foam,
and though the mountains tremble at its tumult.

The LORD of hosts is with us;
the God of Jacob is our stronghold.

There is a river whose streams make glad the city
of God, the holy habitation of the Most High.

God is in the midst of her;
she shall not be overthrown;
God shall help her at the break of day.

The nations make much ado, and the kingdoms
    are shaken;
God has spoken, and the earth shall melt away.

The LORD of hosts is with us;
the God of Jacob is our stronghold.

Come now and look upon the works of the LORD,
what awesome things he has done on earth.

It is he who makes war to cease in all the world;
he breaks the bow, and shatters the spear,
and burns the shields with fire.

"Be still, then, and know that I am God;
I will be exalted among the nations;
I will be exalted in the earth."

The LORD of hosts is with us;
the God of Jacob is our stronghold.

GOSPEL READING

HEAR THE WORD OF THE LORD: Jesus said, "The
lamp of the body is the eye. It follows that if your
eye is clear, your whole body will be filled with
light. But if your eye is diseased, your whole body
will be darkness. If then, the light inside you is
darkened, what darkness that will be! No one can
be the slave of two masters: he will either hate the
first and love the second, or be attached to the
first and despise the second. You cannot be the
slave both of God and of money. That is why I am
telling you not to worry about your life and what
you are to eat, nor about your body and what you
are to wear. Surely life is more than food, and the
body more than clothing! Look at the birds in the
sky. They do not sow or reap or gather into barns;

yet your heavenly Father feeds them. Are you not worth much more than they are? Can any of you, however much you worry, add one single cubit to your span of life?"

—Matthew 6:22–27

SILENCE

PRAYERS OF THE SAINTS

St. Elizabeth often had visions of heaven as she prayed. One day in Lent, she recounted: "I saw the heavens opened, and Jesus leaning toward me in the most kind way, showing me his loving face. I was filled with indescribable joy; and then when his face was gone from my sight, I mourned. Then, he must have taken pity on me, for his face returned before my eyes. He said, 'If you wish to be with me, I will be with you.' And I replied, 'I want nothing to ever separate me from you!'"

—St. Elizabeth of Hungary (d. 1231)

COLLECT

Blessed Father,
may we show ourselves to be faithful.
Our effort here is brief,
the reward eternal.
May the excitements of the world
vanish like a shadow,
and not disturb us.
Amen.

—St. Clare of Assisi

MORNING PRAYER
Saturday
(Theme/Intent: Redefining Family)

PREPARATION

Set your heart on the concerns of your Father.
Open your mind to the truth of your Brother.
Listen for the promptings of your Spirit.
Amen.

GOSPEL SENTENCE

OUR LORD, JESUS CHRIST, SAYS: "I shall no longer
call you servants, because a servant does not know
the master's business; I call you friends, because I
have made known to you everything I have learnt
from my Father."

—John 15:15

SILENCE

CONFESSION

Psalm 51:1–7

Have mercy on me, O God,
    according to your loving-kindness;
in your great compassion blot out my offenses.

Wash me through and through from my wickedness
and cleanse me from my sin.

For I know my transgressions,
and my sin is ever before me.

Against you only have I sinned
and done what is evil in your sight.

And so you are justified when you speak
and upright in your judgment.

Indeed, I have been wicked from my birth,
a sinner from my mother's womb.

For behold, you look for truth deep within me,
and will make me understand wisdom secretly.

For just as the body is one and has many members, and all the members of the body, though many, are one body, so it is with Christ. For in the one Spirit we were all baptized into one body—Jews or Greeks, slaves or free—and we were all made to drink of one Spirit. Indeed, the body does not consist of one member but of many. If one member suffers, all suffer together with it; if one member is honored, all rejoice together with it.

—1 Corinthians 12:12–14, 26

PSALM 150
Laudate Dominum

Hallelujah!
Praise God in his holy temple;
praise him in the firmament of his power.

Praise him for his mighty acts;
praise him for his excellent greatness.

Praise him with the blast of the ram's-horn;
praise him with lyre and harp.

Praise him with timbrel and dance;
praise him with strings and pipe.

Praise him with resounding cymbals;
praise him with loud-clanging cymbals.

Let everything that has breath
praise the LORD.
Hallelujah!

GOSPEL READING

HEAR THE WORD OF THE LORD: He was still speaking to the crowds when suddenly his mother and his brothers were standing outside and were anxious to have a word with him. But to the man who told him this Jesus replied, "Who is my mother? Who are my brothers?" And stretching out his hand towards his disciples he said, "Here are my mother and my brothers. Anyone who does the will of my Father in heaven is my brother and sister and mother."

—Matthew 12:46–50

SILENCE

PRAYERS OF THE SAINTS

Blessed lover of humanity, bless all your people. Send into our hearts the peace of heaven, and grant us also peace in this life. Let no sin prevail among us. Deliver those who are in trouble. Set captives free. Give hope to the hopeless and help to the helpless. Lift the fallen, for you are the haven of the shipwrecked.

—Liturgy of St. Mark

COLLECT

O God, poured out in all of creation,
enlighten us by the splendor of created things.
Give eloquence to our dumbness
that we may praise you.
Open our eyes and alert the ears of our spirit
so that in all creatures we may see, hear, praise, love,
and worship you.

EVENING PRAYER
Saturday
(Theme/Intent: Redefining Family)

PREPARATION

Know this: The LORD himself is God;
he himself has made us, and we are his;
we are his people and the sheep of his pasture.
—Psalm 100:2

GOSPEL SENTENCE

OUR LORD, JESUS CHRIST, SAYS: "Blessed are
those who hunger and thirst for uprightness: they
shall have their fill. Blessed are the merciful: they
shall have mercy shown them."

—Matthew 5:6–7

SILENCE

CONFESSION
Psalm 51:1, 8–19

Have mercy on me, O God,
   according to your loving-kindness;
in your great compassion blot out my offenses.

Purge me from my sin, and I shall be pure;
wash me, and I shall be clean indeed.

Make me hear of joy and gladness,
that the body you have broken may rejoice.

Hide your face from my sins
and blot out all my iniquities.

Create in me a clean heart, O God,
and renew a right spirit within me.

Cast me not away from your presence
and take not your holy Spirit from me.

Give me the joy of your saving help again
and sustain me with your bountiful Spirit.

I shall teach your ways to the wicked,
and sinners shall return to you.

Deliver me from death, O God,
and my tongue shall sing of your righteousness,
O God of my salvation.

Open my lips, O Lord,
and my mouth shall proclaim your praise.

Had you desired it, I would have offered sacrifice,
but you take no delight in burnt-offerings.

The sacrifice of God is a troubled spirit;
a broken and contrite heart, O God, you will not
despise.

Be favorable and gracious to Zion,
and rebuild the walls of Jerusalem.

FIRST READING

I therefore, the prisoner in the Lord, beg you to lead a life worthy of the calling to which you have been called, with all humility and gentleness, with patience, bearing with one another in love, making every effort to maintain the unity of the Spirit in the bond of peace. There is one body and one Spirit, just as you were called to the one hope of your calling, one Lord, one faith, one baptism, one God and Father of all, who is above all and through all and in all.

—Ephesians 4:1–6

PSALM 133
Ecce, quam bonum!

Oh, how good and pleasant it is,
when brethren live together in unity!

It is like fine oil upon the head
that runs down upon the beard,

Upon the beard of Aaron,
and runs down upon the collar of his robe.

It is like the dew of Hermon
that falls upon the hills of Zion.

For there the LORD has ordained the blessing:
life for evermore.

HEAR THE WORD OF THE LORD: Then the mother of Zebedee's sons came with her sons to make a request of [Jesus], and bowed low; and he said to her, "What is it you want?" She said to him, "Promise that these two sons of mine may sit one at your right hand and the other at your left in your kingdom." Jesus answered, "You do not know what you are asking." . . . When the other ten heard this they were indignant with the two brothers. But Jesus called them to him and said, "You know that among the gentiles the rulers lord it over them, and great men make their authority felt. Among you this is not to happen. No; anyone who wants to become great among you must be your servant, and anyone who wants to be first among you must be your slave, just as the Son of man came not to be served but to serve, and to give his life as a ransom for many."

—Matthew 20:20–22, 24–28

SILENCE

I beg you, in the name of the Lord, to always include me in your holy prayers. I am your servant, lowly as I am, and with the sisters of San Damiano, we are devoted to you in prayer. May we all experience the mercy of Jesus Christ, now, and the everlasting vision of heaven, to come.

—St. Clare of Assisi

COLLECT

Heavenly Lord,
bless us,
who follow in the footsteps of your Son, the
   Christ;
bless us,
who listen to the leading of your sweet Spirit;
bless us,
who, with you, are ever renewing the Creation.
Amen.

III
OCCASIONAL PRAYERS OF
St. Clare

ON THE LOVELINESS OF CHRIST

She is happy who clings wholeheartedly to Him:
whose tender touch and kindness,
whose ever fresh remembrance and fragrance,
whose radiant visage and clarity,
continually shares heavenly joy with her and all of
    the citizens
of the heavenly city.
She is happy who clings wholeheartedly to Him!

—Clare of Assisi

ON FAITHFULNESS TO IDEALS

Father of Mercies,
may we strive to always imitate the way
of holy simplicity, humility, and poverty,
shown us by our father, Francis,
    and in our conversion by Christ.
Spread the fragrance of a good name,
from those who live faithfully according to your will.
May we love one another with the charity of Christ.
May the love that we have in our hearts show
itself in our actions.
And may our love and example increase
love of God and charity for one another in all places.
Amen.

—Clare of Assisi

THREE MORE COLLECTS FOR
FAITHFULNESS

GRACEFUL GOD, to whom we have promised ourselves until death: Let us rejoice in the strenuous paths of virtue. Guide us on the path of faithfulness, so that, at the end of our earthly journey, we may be crowned by you with the laurel of life. Amen.

GOD OF LIGHT, eternal and bright-shining, do not allow the noises and shadows of this fleeting world to confuse us. Do not allow the deceptions of the world to muddle us. Give us strength to willingly bear and face the evil that we encounter, and do not allow your provident goodness to puff us up. The faith that you promised us, God, faithfully render it, and we will repay you. Amen.

O GOD, through your blessed son, our Savior Jesus Christ, heaven beckons us. Our Lord made the path on which we, too, will follow him into glory. We seek to love Jesus, who was crucified, with our whole heart, and never allow his memory to escape our minds. Remind us and show us how to meditate always on the mysteries of the cross and the anguish of the mother standing under it. Amen.   —Clare of Assisi

THE OFFICE OF THE FIVE WOUNDS OF CHRIST

THOMAS OF CELANO'S LEGEND OF ST. CLARE tells us that Clare prayed these prayers, taught to her by St. Francis himself. We do not know their origin, and the earliest edition of the text is only as old as the sixteenth century. It is the method of these prayers, rather than the actual words of them, that communicate most profoundly how intimately Francis and Clare sought to identify with the life of Christ.

Each short prayer is addressed to the crucified body of Christ from right to left, hand to foot, and concludes with the wound in his side.

TO THE RIGHT HAND

Precious Lord Jesus, by this sacred wound you have granted me pardon for my sins. Give me the grace to venerate your precious death and these sacred wounds as I should, and grant that by your holy help I may humble my body enough to thank you for this great gift. Amen.

TO THE LEFT HAND

Sweet Lord Jesus, I praise you for the sacred wound of your left hand. You have shown me your mercy; now, I plead, change in me whatever is not pleasing to you. Free me from my enemies and make me worthy of your glory. Amen.

TO THE RIGHT FOOT

Honeyed Lord Jesus, I praise you for the sacred wound of your right foot. Keep me, your humble servant, in your perfect will and deliver me from difficulty. When my life must end, I pray that you will welcome me into eternal joy. Amen.

TO THE LEFT FOOT

Tender Lord Jesus, I praise you for the sacred wound of your left foot. I plead with you, most holy Christ, that I may deserve to receive the Sacrament of your sweet Body and Blood, with an intimate confession and perfect penance, before the day of my death. Amen.

TO THE WOUND IN HIS SIDE

Kind Lord Jesus, I praise you for the sacred wound in your side. By your bitter death, you have cleansed me. Now, strengthen me so that I may love you as I should. May I please you perfectly, now and always. Amen.

FOR AN INCREASE IN FRANCISCAN SPIRITUAL VALUES

Father of our Lord Jesus Christ, we bend our knees and we ask that through the prayers of the glorious Virgin Mary, the holy mother of Christ, and by Father Francis and all of the saints, may Christ, who has given us bountiful beginnings, increase our efforts more and more, and guide us to persevere in that original spirit. Amen.

—Clare of Assisi

CLARE'S BLESSINGS

May You Reflect the Glory of the Lord

May you reflect the glory of the Lord. Place your heart in the divine substance through contemplation. Transform your being into the image that we reflect, the Godhead Itself. Then, you will feel what love is. Then, you will feel the sweetness that is revealed to us through the Spirit, what no eye has seen and no ear has heard, the love that God has for His lovers.   —Clare of Assisi

A Blessing of St. Francis

Made famous in St. Francis's letter to Brother Leo, Francis wrote this blessing on Mt. La Verna in 1224 just after his stigmata experience. The original is still preserved in Assisi today. Francis was simply quoting the Torah (Num. 6:24–26) in his fatherly message for Leo.

The LORD bless you and keep you;
the LORD make his face to shine upon you, and be
    gracious to you;
the LORD lift up his countenance upon you, and
    give you peace.

FROM CLARE'S FINAL WORDS

The Simple Blessing of St. Clare
(To be said upon waking.)
Blessed be you,
God,
who created me.

The Benediction of St. Clare
Now, go calmly in peace,
for you have a good escort.
He who created you
has sent the Holy Spirit who guards
you as a mother does tenderly
love her child.
Amen.

Clare's Last Wish
O daughters,
can you see the
King of Glory
that I see?

IV
OTHER PRAYERS

DEVOTION
to the Virgin Mary

ST. CLARE WAS GREATLY DEVOTED TO THE VIRGIN MARY for many reasons. The Blessed Mother was the virgin of all virgins and the Mother of God. Also, like St. Francis before her, Clare always sought to understand how we are called to give birth to God in our lives. Both Francis and Clare embraced the Mother of Jesus with tremendous love, as Thomas of Celano says in his second *Life of Francis,* because she made the Lord of Majesty into our brother. Finally, Clare's movement was born on that eventful Monday evening during Holy Week—when she fled her family home and joined Francis and the first friars—in the little chapel known as St. Mary of the Angels, or, Portiuncula. When she knelt for Francis to cut her long hair as an entrance into the monastic life, Clare was kneeling before an altar devoted to Mary.

The Magnificat

THIS REMARKABLE SONG OF THE VIRGIN MARY, first said by her just after the Annunciation, has been precious to Christians of all backgrounds for two thousand years. Clare and the first Poor Clares would have prayed it aloud each day.

My soul magnifies the Lord,
and my spirit rejoices in God my Savior,
for he has looked with favor on the lowliness of
    his servant.
Surely, from now on all generations will call me
    blessed;
for the Mighty One has done great things for me,
and holy is his name.
His mercy is for those who fear him
from generation to generation.
He has shown strength with his arm;
he has scattered the proud in the thoughts of their
    hearts.
He has brought down the powerful from their
    thrones,
and lifted up the lowly;
he has filled the hungry with good things,
and sent the rich away empty.
He has helped his servant Israel,
in remembrance of his mercy,
according to the promise he made to our ancestors,
to Abraham and to his descendants forever.

—Luke 1:46–55

The Memorare

ANOTHER POPULAR MEDIEVAL PRAYER TO THE VIRGIN, the Memorare is often associated with St. Bernard of Clairvaux, but its author is actually unknown. *Memorare* is Latin for the first word, "remember."

Remember, O most gracious Virgin Mary,
that never was it known that anyone who fled to
   your protection,
implored your help, or sought your intercession
was left unaided by you.
Inspired with this confidence, I fly to you,
Mary, Virgin of virgins, Mother of Jesus Christ;
to you do I come; before you I stand,
sinful, sorrowful, and trembling.
O Mistress of the World and
   Mother of the Word Incarnate,
despise not my petitions,
but in your mercy hear and answer wretched me
crying to you in this vale of tears.
Be near me, I ask you, in all my necessities,
now and always, and especially at the hour of my
   death.
O clement, O loving, O sweet Virgin Mary.
Amen.

Hail, Lady, Holy Queen

THOMAS OF CELANO'S SECOND *LIFE OF ST. FRANCIS* refers to the saint's love for the Virgin Mary because "she made the Lord of Majesty our brother." In other words, Mary is our mother, too. In the second portion of this prayer of devotion, Francis summarizes some of the most popular medieval metaphors for the Virgin.

Hail, Lady, holy Queen,
holy Mother of God,
virgin made church,
chosen by the Father in heaven,
consecrated by His beloved Son,
through the Holy Spirit, the Paraclete,
in whom there was and always will be
grace abounding and all goodness.

Hail, God's palace,
God's tabernacle,
God's home,
God's robe,
God's servant!
Hail, God's Mother!

FRANCIS'S PSALM
for Those Who Have Gone Before Us

IN CHAPTER 3 OF HIS EARLIEST RULE, St. Francis instructs his brothers on how and what to pray. Among other psalms, he asks them to say Psalm 130, or "the Out of the Depths" along with the Our Father each day for the deceased. The psalm is a lovely, short, ancient psalm of David, and an important piece of the Franciscan liturgical tradition. Reflecting upon death and the fleetingness of life, it is most appropriate to pray, "My soul waits for the LORD, more than watchmen for the morning, more than watchmen for the morning."

Out of the depths have I called to you,
O LORD; LORD, hear my voice;
let your ears consider well the voice of my
    supplication.

If you, LORD, were to note what is done amiss,
O LORD, who could stand?

For there is forgiveness with you;
therefore you shall be feared.

I wait for the LORD; my soul waits for him;
in his word is my hope.

My soul waits for the LORD,
more than watchmen for the morning,
more than watchmen for the morning.

O Israel, wait for the LORD,
for with the LORD there is mercy;

With him there is plenteous redemption,
and he shall redeem Israel from all their sins.

FRANCIS'S
Canticle of the Creatures

ST. FRANCIS WROTE THIS HYMN, taught his friends to sing it, and then asked them to sing it to him on his deathbed. In fact, he composed the Canticle while visiting St. Clare at San Damiano. Francis was in pain, en route to visit a physician in the nearby town of Rieti, when he asked his brothers to take him to see Clare on the way. She prepared a comfortable place for him in the garden, and it is there that Francis wrote this song. It marks the beginning of our modern understanding of how earth and heaven join; it also illustrates how all are called to mediate justice and peace, curb the power of the world, and finally, embrace death as a natural part of life.

Most high, almighty, good Lord God,
to you belong all praise, glory, honor, and blessing!
All my praise to you, Lord God, with all your creatures,
and especially our Brother Sun,
who brings us the day and who brings us the light.
He is fair and shines with a very great splendor:
Lord, he signifies you to us!
All my praise to you, Lord, for our Brother Wind,
and for air and cloud, calms and all weather
through which you uphold life in all creatures.
All my praise, Lord, for our Sister Water,

who is very useful to us and humble
and precious and clean.
All my praise, Lord, for our Brother Fire,
through whom you give us light in the darkness.
He is bright and pleasant and very mighty and strong.
All my praise, Lord, for our Mother Earth,
who sustains us and keeps us,
and brings forth many fruits and flowers
of many colors, and grass.
All my praise, Lord, for all those who pardon one
another for your sake,
and who endure weakness and tribulation.
Blessed are they who peaceably endure, for you,
Most High,
shall give them a crown.
All my praise, Lord, for our Sister Death of the Body,
from whom no one may escape.
Woe to those who die in mortal sin.
and blessed are they who are found walking by
your most holy will,
for the second death
shall have no power to do them any harm.
All praise and blessing, my Lord.
I give you all thanks and serve you with great humility.

SHORT PRAYER POEMS
of Jacopone of Todi

JACOPONE OF TODI was one of the most important Franciscan friars from the century after St. Francis. His songs of love are the essence of the early Franciscan spirit. In the years after St. Clare's death, Jacopone's verses galvanized the movement known as the "Spirituals"—those who taught extreme poverty and simplicity in imitation of Francis and Clare.

His *Laude* poems anticipate the personal, confessional, spiritual struggling of modern writers, and his long poem, *Donna del Paradiso*, portrays Mary the Mother of God with great sensitivity. The latter became the most loved Italian poem of the pre-Renaissance period.

SELECTIONS FROM JACOPONE'S *LAUDE*

Song of the Ecstatic Soul
The activity of the mind
is lulled to rest;
rapt in God,
it can no longer find itself.
Being so deeply engulfed

in that ocean,
now it can find no place
to begin.

Of itself it cannot think,
nor can it say what it is like:
because transformed,
it has another garment.

All its perceptions
have gone forth
to gaze upon the Good,
and contemplate Beauty which has no likeness.

Secrets of the Mystic Life

The doors are flung wide:
When we are joined to God,
we possess
all that is in Him.

We feel what has never been felt,
see what we have not known,
possess what we did not believe,
and taste, though not savor.

Since the soul is entirely lost
to itself,
it possesses a height
of unmeasured perfection.

Since it has not kept
in itself the mixture
of any other thing,
it has received in abundance.

Goodness Unimagined

Above all other language—love,
goodness unimagined,
light without measure
shines in my heart.

Song of a Soul

O why did you create me,
great God of Heaven above?
Redeem me, and await me,
through Jesus Christ my love.

See the Bloom

When Christ is grafted on the spray,
All the withered wood is cut away.
See the bloom springing from decay!
Changed into a wonderful unity.

And so, I live—yet not my self alone;
I am me, yet I am not mine own.
And this change, cross-wise, obscure, unknown—
Words cannot tell.

What Poverty Has

Poverty has nothing in her hand,
nothing craved, in sea, or sky, or land;
she has the Universe at her command.
In the heart of freedom ever-dwelling.

To Love

Born of fire divine,
spun of laughter,
wholly given,
never done.

Running over,
gently entering,
Thy table is
long and wide.

How welcome
we feel
who enter in.

JACOPONE'S VERSE-PRAYERS are always returning
to the central themes of Sts. Francis and Clare.
This one imagines that we, too, stand before
the Nativity. The blessing promised in the last
stanza is an example of the warmth of
Franciscan spirituality.

Your Heart's Desire
All you sinners, erring throng,
serving evil lords so long,
come and hail the Infant Birth!

Even humble men, and innocent,
upright women, the diligent,
come before Him, come and sing.

Do not let Him in vain entreat,
come and kneel before His feet,
giving glory to the King.

You shall have your heart's desire,
tasting, with the heavenly choir,
feasts of Love eternally.

THE STABAT MATER DOLOROSA

THIS PRAYER POEM has been an important part of
Franciscan spirituality since it was first written by
Jacopone of Todi in the century after St. Clare's
death. Both Sts. Francis and Clare consciously
modeled their lives after Christ and his Blessed
Mother; they not only were devoted to Mary, but
they sought to imitate her.

The Stabat Mater Dolorosa
The grieving mother stood weeping,
Near the cross her station keeping

Whereon hung her Son and Lord;
Through whose spirit sympathizing,
Sorrowing and agonizing,
  Also passed the cruel sword.

Oh! how mournful and distressed
Was that favored and most blessed
  Mother of the only Son,
Trembling, grieving, bosom heaving,
While perceiving, scarce believing,
  Pains of that Illustrious One!

Who the man, who, called a brother,
Would not weep, saw he Christ's mother
  In such deep distress and wild?
Who could not sad tribute render
Witnessing that mother tender
  Agonizing with her child?

For his people's sins atoning,
Him she saw in torments groaning,
  Given to the scourger's rod;
Saw her darling offspring dying,
Desolate, forsaken, crying.
  Yield his spirit up to God.

Make me feel thy sorrow's power,
That with thee I tears may shower,
  Tender mother, fount of love!
Make my heart with love unceasing

Burn toward Christ the Lord, that pleasing
　I may be to him above.

Holy mother, this be granted,
That the slain one's wounds be planted
　Firmly in my heart to bide.
Of him wounded, all astounded—
Depths unbounded for me sounded—
　All the pangs with me divide.

Make me weep with thee in union;
With the Crucified, communion
　In his grief and suffering give;
Near the cross, with tears unfailing,
I would join thee in thy wailing
　Here as long as I shall live.

Maid of maidens, all excelling!
Be not bitter, me repelling;
　Make thou me a mourner too;
Make me bear about Christ's dying,
Share his passion, shame defying;
　All his wounds in me renew.
Wound for wound be there created;
With the cross intoxicated
　For thy Son's dear sake, I pray—
May I, fired with pure affection,
Virgin, have through thy protection
　In the solemn Judgment Day.

Let me by the cross be warded,
By the death of Christ be guarded,
  Nourished by divine supplies.
When the body death hath riven,
Grant that to the soul be given
  Glories bright of Paradise.

THE LORD'S PRAYER
in Early Franciscan Tradition

THE LORD'S PRAYER was central to St. Clare's spirituality. In *The Mirror of Perfection*, St. Francis teaches his brothers to pray the Our Father, and he instructs them to praise the Lord both before and after the words of the prayer. In addition, the following commentary—added by Francis to the traditional words of the prayer from Matthew 6—would have been well known by Clare and her sisters.

The Lord's Prayer
(Francis's expanded version)

OUR FATHER,
Most Holy, our Creator and Redeemer, our Savior and our Comforter.

WHO ART IN HEAVEN:
Together with the angels and the saints, giving them light so that they may have knowledge of you, because you, Lord, are Light; inflaming them so that they may love, because you, Lord, are Love; living continually in them and filling them so that they may be happy, because you, Lord, are the supreme good, the eternal good, and it is from you that all good comes, and without you there is no good.

HALLOWED BE THY NAME.

May our knowledge of you become ever clearer, so that we may realize the width and breadth of your blessings, the steadfastness of your promises, the sublimity of your majesty and the depth of your judgments.

THY KINGDOM COME,

So that you may reign in us by your grace and bring us to your Kingdom, where we will see you clearly, love you perfectly, be blessed in your presence, and enjoy you forever.

THY WILL BE DONE IN EARTH
AS IT IS IN HEAVEN:

So that we may love you with our whole heart by always thinking of you; directing our whole intention with our whole mind towards you and seeking your glory in everything; spending all our powers and affections of soul and body with all our strength in the service of your love alone. May we also love our neighbors as ourselves, encouraging them to love you as best we can, rejoicing at the good fortune of others, just as if it were our own, and sympathizing with their misfortunes, giving offense to no one.

GIVE US THIS DAY OUR DAILY BREAD,

Your own beloved Son, our Lord Jesus Christ, so to remind us of the love he showed for us and to help us understand and appreciate it and everything that he did or said or suffered.

AND FORGIVE US OUR TRESPASSES,

In your infinite mercy, and by the power of the Passion of your Son, our Lord Jesus Christ, together with the merits and the intercession of the Blessed Virgin Mary and all your saints.

AS WE FORGIVE
THOSE WHO TRESPASS AGAINST US,
And if we do not forgive perfectly, Lord, make us do so, so that we may indeed love our enemies out of our love for you, and pray fervently to you for them, never returning evil for evil, anxious only to serve everybody in you.

AND LEAD US NOT INTO TEMPTATION.
Neither hidden nor obvious, sudden, or unforeseen.

BUT DELIVER US FROM EVIL—
Present, past, or to come.
Amen.

N.ERICHSEN.

V
APPENDICES

A VERY BRIEF LIFE
of
St. Agnes of Rome
(d. 304)

BOTH ST. AMBROSE AND ST. AUGUSTINE, two of the Latin Church Fathers, speak of St. Agnes of Rome in their writings. They tell us that St. Agnes was only thirteen when she was martyred, probably in the year 304, during the hideous persecutions under the Roman Emperor Diocletian. Hers is one of the first stories of a virgin martyr.

Early Christian tradition is replete with stories such as St. Agnes's, and these stories were terribly important to St. Clare and her own understanding of embracing Christ. Agnes spurned the offers of men who were drawn only by her physical beauty, and she opted instead for a "marriage" to Christ. Agnes's suitors were angered and humiliated by her refusals of marriage, and so they brought to the local governor accusations against her for being a Christian.

Father Alban Butler, the great eighteenth-century chronicler of saints' lives, recounts what happened next:

> The judge at first employed the mildest expressions and most seductive promises, to

which Agnes paid no regard, repeating always that she could have no other spouse but Jesus Christ. He then made use of threats, but found her endowed with a masculine courage, and even eager to suffer torment and death. At last terrible fires were made, and iron hooks, racks and other instruments of torture displayed before her, with threats of immediate execution. The heroic child surveyed them undismayed, and made good cheer in the presence of the fierce and cruel executioners. . . .

The governor, seeing his measures ineffectual, said he would send her to a house of prostitution, where what she prized so highly should be exposed to the insults of the brutal and licentious youth of Rome. Agnes answered that Jesus Christ was too jealous of the purity of His chosen ones to suffer it to be violated in such a manner, for He was their defender and protector. "You may," said she, "stain your sword with my blood, but you will never be able to profane my body, consecrated to Christ." The governor was so incensed at this that he ordered her to be immediately led to the place of shame with liberty to all to abuse her person at pleasure.

Many young profligates ran thither, full of wicked desires, but were seized with such awe at the sight of the saint that they durst not approach her; one only excepted, who, attempting to be rude to her, was that very instant, by a flash, as it were of lightning from Heaven, struck blind, and fell trembling to the ground. His companions, terrified, took him up and carried him to Agnes, who was singing hymns of praise to Christ, her protector. The virgin by prayer restored his sight and his health.

[Then,] the governor . . . was highly exasperated to see himself set at defiance by one of her tender age and sex. . . . [H]e condemned her to be beheaded. Agnes, filled with joy on hearing this sentence, "went to the place of execution more cheerfully," says St. Ambrose, "than others go to their wedding." The spectators shed tears to see this beautiful child loaded with fetters, and offering herself fearlessly to the sword of the executioner, who with trembling hand cut off her head at one stroke. Her body was buried at a short distance from Rome, beside the Nomentan road.

Less than fifty years later, a basilica was erected on the site of St. Agnes's burial site in Rome, under the supervision of Constantina, daughter of the first Christian Roman Emperor, Constantine. The fame of Agnes spread rapidly. She was recognized as a martyr/saint throughout the Middle Ages. Her feast day is January 21.

The heroic story of St. Agnes of Rome inspired many early Franciscan women. St. Clare's younger sister, Catarina, joined Clare only sixteen days after Clare's own conversion, becoming the second Franciscan woman. Eventually, Catarina took Agnes as her religious name, and she is known to history as St. Agnes of Assisi. Similarly, the disciple with whom Clare often corresponded, Agnes of Prague, took St. Agnes of Rome as her patron saint and was, in turn, herself canonized in 1989 by Pope John Paul II.

"Sister Clare,"
A "LITTLE PLAY" BY LAURENCE HOUSMAN

LAURENCE HOUSMAN lived one hundred years ago and wrote dozens of one-act plays about events in the life of St. Francis of Assisi. They were published singly beginning in 1922, and then eventually in three small volumes. This collection was called *Little Plays of Saint Francis: Complete Edition* (1935) and included the play that follows, *Sister Clare.*

The freshness and vitality of *Sister Clare* remains unaltered today. The play captures the simplicity and joy of the early Franciscan movement in ways that are not possible in either contemporary biographies or medieval texts. Sts. Francis and Clare play the key parts in the drama, but Brother Juniper also offers some spontaneous and characteristic moments of foolishness. The result is a timeless and moving portrait of what may have happened on that first night of Clare's joining the friars at Portiuncula. I have only slightly modernized the language of the original, and have cut the length by approximately one quarter.

SISTER CLARE
BY LAURENCE HOUSMAN

THE SETTING: In a bare, stable-like interior, Brother Juniper sits by a fire of glowing embers, his head dropping with sleep. To one side of the fire is a rough bench, to the other a recessed corn-bin with half-doors, the upper of which stands ajar. Opposite the fireplace, stairs lead up to a hayloft. Beside the staircase is a door into another chamber; the outer door is at the back. From within comes Brother Bernard carrying a light, and stands for a moment watching Brother Juniper's jerky efforts to keep awake.

BERNARD: Why aren't you in bed, brother?

JUNIPER: The father said I was to wait up.

BERNARD: Oh? Where is he?

JUNIPER: Gone into the forest to fetch wood.

BERNARD: At this time of night? What for?

JUNIPER: Brother Fire sent him for it. I heard 'em talking. The father said: "Brother Fire, it's late. Won't you go to sleep?" "No," said Brother Fire, and stuck out his tongue. "I won't." "What, you're staying awake?" said the father. "I am," he said, and again stuck out his tongue. So Brother Fire got his way and the father's gone to fetch wood for him.

BERNARD: Has he been gone long?

JUNIPER: If I've been sleeping, he perhaps has. [He

turns toward the fire.] May you end!—
sending the father out like that, on a cold
night!

BERNARD: If the father doesn't mind, why should
you?

JUNIPER: If we waited all minding until the father
did, we might never mind anything!

BERNARD: Very true, brother. But why did you have
to stay up after all the others?

JUNIPER: He said we had a friend coming, and if he
wasn't back, Brother Fire and I were to be
here, to make things comfortable.

BERNARD *[smiling]*: So Brother Fire had a reason?

JUNIPER: Sure! I never thought of it. There! *[To the
fire:]* I forgive you, then! *[He puts on the last log.]*
Oh! When Father Francis comes   back, he'll find
me sitting up in spirit, maybe, but in the body I will
be—*[a snore comes from the loft]*—like the rest of us
up there.

[Falling asleep, Juniper jerks, and is then awake again.]

BERNARD *[going toward the stairs]*:

God give you good sleep, Brother Juniper.

JUNIPER: Yes, if God sends it to me! But more times
than not it seems to come from the Devil.

BERNARD: Why do you say that?

JUNIPER: Because when I'm asleep, I dream of
things I should not.

BERNARD: So do we all. But on waking, finding that
they are not real, we forget them.

JUNIPER: Yeah? Do we? I wish I did. Oh, women are

my mischief! I came here to be away from
them. But Lord! When you go to sleep
there's generally one waiting for you.

BERNARD: Come, come, brother.

JUNIPER: It is so! Have you heard, brother, how one
day, just through lying asleep on his side—
or his back, maybe—Adam got loose of a
rib and it turned into a woman?

BERNARD: Surely.

JUNIPER: So that's how sin came into the world—all
because of Adam's sleeping.

BERNARD: God caused him to sleep, brother.

JUNIPER: Did he? But he didn't wake when God
called him. "Mother Eve," Brother Elias
told us her name was; and a good name
too, if it stands for evil. Oh, women are
the root of all mischief. You know that
yourself, Brother Bernard.

BERNARD: I have known it, brother. God rest you to
peace, and keep us all from temptation.

*[He goes upstairs, and for a few moments you see his light over
the partition. Then, the light goes out and from above comes
only the restful sound of slumber.]*

JUNIPER: Temptation? Oh, I don't mind temptation,
when it's what you call reasonable. But it's
the unreasonableness of it that takes me
where I'm weakest. Lord! If a temptation
of that kind were to come here now, I
couldn't answer for myself—nor for her
either. *[To the fire:]* Well, are you keeping

awake, or must I? There's no reason for the
two of us doing it. So long as I wait up,
that's all he told me. . . . "Wait up," he
said, "wait up." But when the weight of
waiting gets on your eyes, it's like saying
"Up!" to a dead donkey, for all the heed
they give to you. *[And so, gently admonishing
himself, he drops off to sleep, while from the loft
above come the peaceful snores of the brothers.]*

*[Then, the door opens. Cloaked and hooded, a young girl enters.
There, with all the fresh beauty of saint or sinner, stands Sister
Clare, as, from this day on, she is destined to be known.
Advancing, she then stops and looks at the sleeping Juniper.]*

CLARE: Brother, may I come in and be with you?

*[Juniper wakes with a start, turns, stares at the apparition, crosses
himself with both hands, springs convulsively to his feet, and runs
in haste to the corn-bin. He jumps in and closes the door.]*
*[Unamused and unperturbed, Clare stands looking after him,
then moves to the fire and, stretching out her hands, crouches to
warm herself. But almost at once, her hands fall from weariness.
With a deep sigh of exhaustion she sinks down and lets her head
fall back on the bench.]*
*[Brother Juniper, after a while, peeps out, and not looking low
enough believes that she is gone. He cautiously puts forth a leg.
In doing so, he upsets a stool. Clare opens her eyes and turns.
Juniper whips back into hiding. Quietly but resolutely, without
any movement or speech, she begins to dig him out.]*
CLARE: Brother . . . brother . . . brother.

[Unable to resist, Juniper puts out his head, and stays fixed by the stronger will.]

CLARE: Come back, brother. I would like to speak with you.

JUNIPER *[Very gradually, emerging]*: What are you doing here?

CLARE: Resting.

JUNIPER: What are you resting here for?

CLARE: Because rest is here.

JUNIPER: Not for the likes of you, though. God forbid!

CLARE: God hasn't forbidden it yet, brother.

JUNIPER: What are you calling me "brother" for? I'm no brother to a temptation like you! Oh Lord! Where's Father Francis!

CLARE: In the forest, gathering wood.

JUNIPER: Oh? You knew that, did you? So you thought you'd catch me alone. [He starts to cross himself.] Oh God, be merciful to me a sinner! God be merciful to me a sinner! God be merciful to me a—

CLARE: Once is enough, brother. He hears you.

JUNIPER: When I've seen you go, I'll believe it!

CLARE: If you tell me to go, I will go.

JUNIPER: Surely it's not reasonable of you to say that. But if I don't tell you to go, it's not because I want you to stay.

CLARE: Why shouldn't I stay, brother?

JUNIPER: "Brother" again! What was it that brought you here?

CLARE: A rough road, a dark night, and feet that, in God's keeping, did not fail.

JUNIPER: Oh Lord! Am I waking, or am I sleeping?
           [In saying so, he mounts the stairs to the sleeping
           chamber in great haste, and begins to rouse the brothers.]
           Brother Bernard . . . Brother Bernard,
           wake for the love of God! Brother Giles!
           Brother Elias! Brother Angelo!

BERNARD: What is it, brother?

JUNIPER: Get the others to wake up! When we are
           all awake, I will tell you.

ELIAS: We are awake, brother.

JUNIPER: Are you sure you're awake? I wish I could
           be sure that I was!

BERNARD: Tell us, brother: What is the matter?

JUNIPER: Down below is a temptation, brother,
           waiting for all of you. The Lord save you
           from it—and me—and all of us! Come!
           [The brothers begin to follow.] Strike a light,
           and one of you hold me by the hand, for
           down there it is dark. *[A light is struck; together*
           the brothers descend the stairs, Juniper leading
           them.] Wait now! Cross yourselves; then I'll
           show it to you. Look . . . over there!

[The brothers see dimly through the faint light that there is a
woman, young and fair, stretched out asleep before the fire.]

ELIAS: How did this happen, brother?

JUNIPER: God only knows. I was asleep. When I
           woke up, she was there.

BERNARD: What shall we do, brothers?

GILES: Wait until the little Father returns.

ELIAS: We cannot wait here, brother.

ANGELO: Let us pray, brothers, that we flee from temptation.

ELIAS: Yes, but here is temptation.

GILES: I think that the temptation is asleep, and will not awaken.

ELIAS: In sleep, Brother Giles, does the worm die? In sleep is the fire quenched? Come, let us go!

GILES *[making the sign of the cross over Clare]*: The Lord bless thee, little sister, and give thee peace.

[They go to the door, and opening it encounter Francis, who enters carrying wood.]

Francis: Where are you going, brothers?

JUNIPER: We were going for a walk, father, away from what is over there. *[He points to the sleeper. Francis goes over and looks at her.]*

FRANCIS: Sweet Sister Charity, come at last! . . . Why leave, brothers?

[The brothers stand looking a little ashamed of themselves.]

BERNARD: We were afraid, father.

FRANCIS: Of what?

ELIAS: Of temptation.

FRANCIS: Where, brothers?

BERNARD: In our own hearts, father.

FRANCIS: Come, then, let us sit down, that in our hearts we may find reason. Our little sister is weary and will not wake up.

JUNIPER: Father, was she the friend that I was to wait for?

FRANCIS: Yes, brother.

JUNIPER: But why didn't you tell me, father, that it

was a woman!

FRANCIS: Why should I? You could see that for
yourself.

ELIAS: Father, if you knew that she was coming,
why did you go and leave us?

FRANCIS: Because with Brother Juniper you were safe.

JUNIPER: With me? The Lord save us!

ANGELO: Why has she come, father?

FRANCIS: God sent her.

GILES: To be one of us, father?

FRANCIS: Yes! If we have brothers, why can't we have
sisters, as well? Are we to say "Go away" to
any that have heard the voice of Love say
"Come"?

ELIAS: But what can she do, father?

FRANCIS: Bring others. Work as we do. Give service.
Love poverty. Find freedom. Have joy!

ELIAS: But . . . what will the world say, father?

FRANCIS: I don't know, brother. Must we wait until
we know what the world will say? What
God says we know already. For had God
not called her, she would not have come.

BERNARD: Who is she, father?

FRANCIS: A little sister, named Clare. *[He puts more
wood on the fire, and covers Sister Clare with a
cloak.]* Let us go to bed, brothers; it is late.
You, Brother Fire, will sit up with her, and
you, Sister Cloak, will keep her warm.
Good night, little sister, sleep well.

JUNIPER: Father, you tempt me into thinking that

there is no such thing in the world as a
temptation.

FRANCIS: It's a good thought, brother. Play on it,
and some day it may come true.

JUNIPER: If only Father Adam could have thought
that!

FRANCIS: What then, brother?

JUNIPER: Then the Tree wouldn't have tempted him.

FRANCIS *[happy to be so instructed]*: No! . . . no!

This is true, brothers. Juniper is always right.

GILES: Little Father, he always is!

[Elias makes a quick move of protest, crosses the room, takes up the candle, and stands waiting. The rest of the brothers one by one pass quietly back to bed. Elias follows them. Francis crosses, turns, and motions to Juniper.]

FRANCIS: Come, Juniper!

[And together they all go to the loft to sleep.]

END

INDEX OF NAMES, SUBJECTS, AND SCRIPTURES

NOTES

p. 3. *She chose to run away . . .*
See Appendix B for a dramatic rendering of that first night.

p. 6. *". . . and love of the heavenly life."*
From the essay "St. Clare of Assisi," in *The Romanticism of St. Francis and Other Studies in the Genius of the Franciscans*, by Father Cuthbert, O.S.F.C. (New York: Longmans, Green and Co., 1915), 83-4.

p. 7. *"Clare's Prison."*
Linda Bird Francke, *On the Road with Francis of Assisi: A Timeless Journey through Umbria and Tuscany, and Beyond* (New York: Random House, 2005), chap. 6.

p. 8. *". . . inclined to lust and sensuality."*
Sister Mary Frances Hone, O.S.C., "The Refining of the Light," in *The Cord*; 3.

p. 8. *". . . in truth it was he that was the wind."*
G. K. Chesterton, *Saint Thomas Aquinas: The Dumb Ox* (New York: Sheed and Ward, 1933), 3.

p. 9. *". . . the treasures of heavenly wisdom."*
The Little Flowers, tale 14.

p. 10. *". . . but known throughout the towns."*
Translated and quoted in Catherine Mooney's *Gendered Voices: Medieval Saints and Their Interpreters* (Philadelphia: University of Pennsylvania Press, 1999), 58.

p. 12. *". . . under the transforming action of God."*
Evelyn Underhill, *The School of Charity* (New York: Longmans, Green and Co., 1934), 19.

p. 14. *Thomas writes . . . "a sword will pierce your own soul too."*
Luke 2:34–35; Thomas of Celano, *The Legend*, chap. xxviii.

p. 18. *St. Agnes of Rome.*
See Appendix A for *A Very Brief Life of St. Agnes of Rome.*

p. 19. *Ermentrude of Bruges . . . Thomas of Celano*
Some scholars question the authenticity of Clare's letter to Ermentrude. Also, there is plenty of debate as to who authored *The Legend of St. Clare* in the mid-thirteenth century soon after her death, as part of the process of building the case for her canonization. Some have claimed that it was Brother Mark, the friar who was chaplain to the Sisters at the time of Clare's death. Many other names have also been put forward, particularly in the last century, when Franciscan studies entered the modern era. In both cases, there are equally strong arguments for accepting Clare as author of the letter, and Thomas as author of *The Legend*, and so we will.

p. 19. *. . . the most recent authoritative edition.*
Regis J. Armstrong, O.F.M. Cap, trans., *Clare of Assisi: Early Documents*, rev. ed. (New York: New City Press, 2006).

p. 22. *. . . expectant women were instructed to clutch the books . . . during childbirth . . .*
M. Dominica Legge, *Anglo-Norman Literature and Its Background* (New York: Oxford University Press, 1973), 258.

p. 23. *She never fell in love with Francis.*
See my discussion of this in *Francis and Clare of Assisi: How a Sacred Friendship Brought Light to the Dark Ages* (Brewster, MA: Paraclete Press, 2007).

p. 24–5. *Blessed Angela of Foligno.*
D. 1309.

p. 25. *"I am the Holy Spirit . . . sweet to me."*
Modernized translation my own. See *The Book of Divine Consolation of the Blessed Angela of Foligno*, trans. by Mary G. Steegmann (New York: Cooper Square Publishers, 1966), 160.

p. 25. *". . . the rapture of being possessed."*
Pierre Teilhard de Chardin, *The Prayer of the Universe* (New York: Harper & Row, 1973), 122.

p. 27. *Return to yourself . . . what is beyond you.*
The *Works of Bonaventure, I*, trans. by Jose de Vinck (Paterson, NJ: St. Anthony Guild Press, 1960), 214.

p. 33. *. . . deep enough for elephants to swim.*
Patrick Boyde, *Human Vices and Human Worth in Dante's Comedy* (Cambridge: Cambridge University Press, 2000), 102.

p. 35. *Let him kiss me . . . that conceived me.*
Song of Songs 1:2–3 and 3:4.

p. 36. *Is it nothing to you . . .*
Lamentations 1:12

p. 36. *The thought of my affliction . . .*
Lamentations 3:19–20.

p. 37. *Kings' daughters . . . follow in procession.*
Psalm 45:10–15.

pp. 37–8. *Thomas of Celano immortalized . . .*
The Legend of St. Clare, chap. 5.

p. 39. *"Consider your own call . . ."*
1 Cor. 1:26.

p. 40. *"For you know the generous act . . ."*
2 Cor. 8:9.

p. 41. *"Eating the fruit of a bountiful tree."*
Chapter 37 of Thomas of Celano's *Life*.

p. 48. *"Happy, indeed . . . unceasingly admire."*
Clare of Assisi: Early Documents, 54.

p. 49. *. . . following his footprints closely . . .*
1 Peter 2:21.

p. 55. *Heavenly Father . . . it is you. Amen.*
This prayer is derived from the fourth paragraph of Clare's second letter to Agnes. It also makes reference to Luke 10:42 and Romans 12:1 (as does Clare in that paragraph).

p. 59. *I would die gladly . . . never needs to go very far.*
From *The Flowing Light of the Godhead*, Book II, part 2.

pp. 59–60. *What you are doing . . . spirit of God has called you. Amen.*
Derived (and words only slighted changed) from Clare's second letter to Agnes, paragraph five.

p. 71. *Fear not . . . heart and soul.*
Derived from Angela of Foligno's "Sixth Consolation of the Passion of Jesus Christ," in *The Book of Divine Consolation of the Blessed Angela of Foligno*, 215–8.

p. 73. Now, remember . . . every human being.
Derived from Galatians 1:15–16.

p. 78. *Eternal God . . . blameless as Your Son. Amen.*
Macrina was the sister of Sts. Basil and Gregory of Nyssa. This prayer is taken from the *Life of Macrina*, written by Gregory of Nyssa.

p. 79. *Live always in the truth . . . with the Virgin Mary. Amen.*
According to scholars, this canticle was written at about the same time as the *Canticle of the Creatures*, when Francis was ill at the end of his life and Clare and the sisters were worrying about him. It is one of the "last words" from Francis to the sisters. See *Francis of Assisi: Early Documents, Vol. 1*, ed. by Regis J. Armstrong, et al. (New York: New City Press, 1999), 115. Slight changes have been made for this translation.

p. 84. *May the Lord . . . be it so. Amen.*
This collect is very loosely based on one from the traditional Capuchin Office of St. Clare.

pp. 89–90. *Let us rise . . . Harden not your hearts.*
From St. Benedict's *Rule*, the prologue. The two scriptures quoted are Romans 13:11 and Psalm 95:7–8.

p. 90. *May you have . . . Body of Christ. Amen.*
Derived loosely from Clare's third letter to Agnes, paragraph 3.

p. 96. *May Holy Wisdom . . . friends of God. Amen.*
This collect incorporates language from Clare's fourth letter to Agnes, paragraph four, and phrases from the Apocryphal book The Wisdom of Solomon 7:24–27.

p. 102. *Now . . . use words. Amen.*
This collect is inspired by Galatians 1:15–6, and also incorporates Francis's famous statement about preaching.

p. 103. *I bend my knee. Amen.*
Derived from the Testament of Clare, paragraph 20.

p. 107. *Holy One . . . land of prayer.*
Inspired by, and using phrasing from, Evagrius Ponticus'
Praktikos 61. See *The Praktikos: Chapters on Prayer*, trans.
John Eudes Bamberger (Spencer, MA: Cistercian Studies,
1970), 65.

p. 112. *I adore . . . made beautiful.*
From "Prayer to the Holy Cross."

p. 112. *O God . . . Amen.*
This collect incorporates language from Clare's fourth letter to
Agnes, paragraph one, as well as phrases from Revelation 14:3–4.

p. 113. *Most loving God . . . bless you.*
Derived from Galatians 1:15–16.

p. 117. *A prayer . . . herself with truth.*
From a letter of St. Catherine to Sister Eugenia, Catherine's
niece. This title and translation © Jon M. Sweeney.

p. 119. *You are the Holy One . . . hold together.*
Derived from Colossians 1:15, 17.

p. 125. *Blessed Father . . . disturb us. Amen.*
Derived from the letter to Ermentrude of Bruges, second
paragraph.

p. 130. *O God . . . and worship you.*
Inspired by, and using phrasing from, a passage from St.
Bonaventure's *Soul's Journey into God*. See *Bonaventure: The
Soul's Journey into God, The Tree of Life, The Major Life of
Saint Francis*, trans. Ewert Cousins (New York: Paulist Press,
1978), 67–8.

p. 136. *I beg you . . . heaven, to come.*
Derived from the first letter to Agnes of Prague, last paragraph.

p. 139. *She is happy . . . to Him.*
Derived from the fourth letter to Agnes of Prague, paragraphs 9–14.

p. 139–8. *Father of mercies . . . in all places. Amen.*
Derived from the *Testament* of Clare, paragraph 15.

p. 140. *Graceful God . . . standing under it. Amen.*
These three collects are derived from the first three paragraphs of Clare's letter to Ermentrude of Bruges. Various editions.

pp. 141–2. *Precious Lord Jesus . . . now and always. Amen.*
See *Clare of Assisi: Early Documents*, pp. 422–4 for the most complete explanation of these prayers. My rendering of them is a shortened version of what appears there, and may, in fact, be closer to the version prayed by Francis and Clare.

p. 143. *Father of our Lord . . . original spirit. Amen.*
Derived from the last two paragraphs of Clare's *Testament*.

p. 143. *May you reflect . . . for His lovers.*
This blessing is derived from paragraph 5 of Clare's third letter to Agnes. It also includes references to 2 Corinthians 3:18 and 1 Corinthians 2:9.

p. 144. *Now go calmly . . . love her child. Amen.*
These words were spoken by Clare on her deathbed, speaking to her own soul. In Thomas of Celano's *Life*, Clare says to one of her sisters that she is speaking to her own soul.

p. 147. *Both Francis and Clare . . . into our brother.*
Thomas of Celano, Second *Life*, paragraph 198.

p. 155. *. . . the most loved Italian poem . . .*
The translations that follow are adaptations of those first published in Evelyn Underhill's 1919 study, *Jacopone da Todi, Poet and Mystic: A Spiritual Biography*. The translations for that volume were done by Mrs. Theodore Beck, and have been shortened and revised in the renderings that follow. Underhill viewed Jacopone as one of the most important poets of mystical union with God, a trait that comes through clearly in the first two. In the others, it is also easy to see the way in which the core themes of Franciscan life were carried on by the great poet's songs and verses. The first three poems are derived from *Laude,* xci, and the remaining five are from *Laude*, xcviii, lx, lxxxi, and lxiv, respectively.

pp. 159–62. *Stabat Mater Dolorosa*
Translation by Abraham Coles.

ACKNOWLEDGMENTS

MANY THANKS go to Lil Copan for her fine editorial guidance, and to the design team at Paraclete Press for their usual excellence. In addition, the advice of Sr. Mary Francis Hone, O.S.C., was invaluable in uncovering sources and building themes for the book. Thanks to Sr. Mary, for instance, for pointing out the quote from Teilhard de Chardin that appears on page 25.

The small illustrations throughout the book are taken from *The Story of Assisi*, by Lina Duff Gordon, illustrated by Nelly Ericksen and M. Helen James (London: J. M. Dent & Co., 1901). And the frontispiece of a St. Clare icon is a photograph taken by the author outside the Cathedral of San Rufino in Assisi.

ABOUT PARACLETE PRESS

Who We Are

Paraclete Press is an ecumenical publisher of books and recordings on Christian spirituality. Our publishing represents a full expression of Christian belief and practice—from Catholic to Evangelical, from Protestant to Orthodox.

Paraclete Press is the publishing arm of the Community of Jesus, an ecumenical monastic community in the Benedictine tradition. As such, we are uniquely positioned in the marketplace without connection to a large corporation and with informal relationships to many branches and denominations of faith.

We like it best when people buy our books from booksellers, our partners in successfully reaching as wide an audience as possible.

What We Are Doing
Books

Paraclete Press publishes books that show the richness and depth of what it means to be Christian. Although Benedictine spirituality is at the heart of all that we do, we publish books that reflect the Christian experience across many cultures, time periods, and houses of worship.

We publish books that nourish the vibrant life of the church and its people—books about spiritual practice, formation, history, ideas, and customs.

We have several different series of books within Paraclete Press, including the bestselling Living Library series of modernized classic texts; A Voice from the Monastery—giving voice to men and women monastics about what it means to live a spiritual life today; award-winning literary faith fiction; and books that explore Judaism and Islam and discover how these faiths inform Christian thought and practice.

Recordings

From Gregorian chant to contemporary American choral works, our music recordings celebrate the richness of sacred choral music through the centuries. Paraclete is proud to distribute the recordings of the internationally acclaimed choir Gloriæ Dei Cantores, who have been praised for their "rapt and fathomless spiritual intensity" by *American Record Guide*, and the Gloriæ Dei Cantores Schola, which specializes in the study and performance of Gregorian chant. Paraclete is also the exclusive North American distributor of the recordings of the Monastic Choir of St. Peter's Abbey in Solesmes, France, long considered to be a leading authority on Gregorian chant performance.

Learn more about us at our website:
www.paracletepress.com, or call us toll-free at
1-800-451-5006.

ALSO BY JON SWEENEY

The St. Francis Prayer Book

A Guide to Deepen Your Spiritual Life

164 pages
ISBN 13: 978-1-55725-352-1
$13.95, Deluxe paperback

This warm-hearted little book is a window into the soul of St. Francis, one of the most passionate and inspiring followers of Jesus. "Prayer was to Francis as play is to a child—natural, easy, creative, and joyful," author Jon Sweeney tells us.

With this guide, you will:

•Pray the words that Francis taught his spiritual brothers and sisters to pray.
•Explore Francis's time and place and feel the joy and earnestness of the first Franciscans.
•Experience how it is possible to live a contemplative and active life, at the same time.

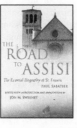

The Road to Assisi

The Essential Biography of St. Francis
by Paul Sabatier
Edited with an Introduction and Annotations by Jon M. Sweeney

208 pages
ISBN 13: 978-1-55725-401-6
$14.95, Trade Paper

A Selection of:
Book of the Month Club
History Book Club
Crossings Book Club
The Literary Guild

Sabatier's classic biography portrays a fully human Francis, with insecurities and fear, but also a gentle mystic and passionate reformer who desired to live as Jesus taught his disciples. This new edition features maps and illustrations, helpful sidebars with additional information, explanatory notes, select tales from the *Little Flowers*, and a complete bibliography.

Available at your local bookstore and
www.paracletepress.com.